D1715468

THE MOST UNLIKELY CHAMPION

A Memoir by
VERA KOO
with Justin Pahl

BALBOA.
PRESS

A DIVISION OF HAY HOUSE

Designed by Amy Swan.

Balboa Press books may be ordered through booksellers or by contacting:

Balboa Press
A Division of Hay House
1663 Liberty Drive
Bloomington, IN 47403
www.balboapress.com
1 (877) 407-4847

Because of the dynamic nature of the Internet, any web addresses or links contained in this book may have changed since publication and may no longer be valid. The views expressed in this work are solely those of the author and do not necessarily reflect the views of the publisher, and the publisher hereby disclaims any responsibility for them.

The author of this book does not dispense medical advice or prescribe the use of any technique as a form of treatment for physical, emotional, or medical problems without the advice of a physician, either directly or indirectly. The intent of the author is only to offer information of a general nature to help you in your quest for emotional and spiritual well-being. In the event you use any of the information in this book for yourself, which is your constitutional right, the author and the publisher assume no responsibility for your actions.

Print information available on the last page.

ISBN: 978-1-5043-8848-1 (sc)
ISBN: 978-1-5043-8849-8 (hc)
ISBN: 978-1-5043-8857-3 (e)

Library of Congress Control Number: 2017914158

Balboa Press rev. date: 11/05/2018

CONTENTS

INTRODUCTION

When Vera Koo enrolled in a firearm safety course at a college in the 1980s, she could not have looked more out of place. She was a petite, middle-aged Chinese-American woman in a class mostly full of men. She had little experience with firearms and took the course to further her knowledge so she would no longer fear guns. Little did she know that safety course would set her on a path to becoming one of the world's most accomplished professional women's shooters.

An immigrant from Hong Kong who was raised under traditional, conservative Chinese values, Koo was taught from an early age that a woman's place is to serve her family and her household. While she strived to uphold the values of her Chinese upbringing, she also carved her own path. Koo became the most unlikely pistol champion. She's an eight-time winner of the women's division of the NRA National Action Pistol Championship, known as the Bianchi Cup. More than an athletic endeavor, Koo's venture into sport shooting became a vehicle that helped her navigate life's challenges. Koo and her husband saw their business teeter on the edge of bankruptcy before they built it back up. She experienced the pain of a parent's worst nightmare when the couple lost their first son. And then, nearly 25 years ago, she endured a personal betrayal that rocked her to her core.

In her debut book, Koo details these events and how she came to deal with them thanks to her faith in God and her passion for sport shooting, which became her therapy.

Koo's response to life's waves of adversity taught her a valuable lesson: The most spectacular rise can only come after you fall.

FOREWORD

When I met Vera Koo, in December 2014, we were both skeptical that I would be able to "tell her story," a goal she'd been working toward for more than a decade. After all, on the surface, Vera and I had little in common. Vera was Chinese-American and nearly 70. She'd been a successful businesswoman, an eight-time sport shooting women's national champion, and a loving, supportive mother to four kids.

Me? I was a middle-class white guy in his late 20s. Neither of us was sure it was going to work.

Then Vera started telling me about her life. It's a quintessentially American story – one about family and business, success and failure, and determination in the face of great odds. Listening to her story, I became certain that there was no story quite like it – and no person remotely like Vera Koo. Her story might be unique, but its scope is universal. Although not everyone knows what it's like to be an immigrant, almost everyone understands how it feels to, in Vera's words, "search for the thing you are good at." Most of us will never be sport-shooting champions, but all of us have adopted new hobbies and wondered how far we might take them. And although most of us hopefully will never lose a child, almost everyone has felt the sting of failure or the pain of lost love.

X

This universality motivated Vera to tell her story. She hopes that people, especially women, will recognize aspects of their lives in hers. As Vera told me the first time we met, "When people look at me, they don't think I'm a champion. They don't think I'm anyone." Her story is a testament to that old truism – looks can be deceiving.

In Vera's case, her slight frame hides the spirit and determination of a champion. The extraordinary woman who emerges throughout the course of this book is the woman I got to know during the two years we spent working together. Vera's incredible determination is matched only by her kindness and generosity. (Most of her friends attest to this fact: Vera is famous for bringing gifts whenever she visits someone. And every time we met up for work – in a hotel lobby or restaurant – she knew every employee by name. She always wanted to know about how their day was going.) Although she's accomplished things she never dreamed were possible, she hasn't lost her sense of humility – an inheritance from her mother – or her self-deprecating humor. Writing a memoir suggests a degree of hubris, and yet Vera has almost no ego. She works tirelessly and is quick to joke about herself. Her stories, even of difficult times, are not just funny, but told with the warmth of someone who loves people and life.

Capturing the heart of these stories, as well as Vera's unique voice, was the most important part of our work together. Vera's life has taken her from Hong Kong to San Francisco, from working mother to world champion; it's had more twists and turns than a great novel. My greatest fear was not doing that story justice. I think the work we've done has captured not just Vera's essence but also the incredible arc of her life.

The more time I spent with Vera, the more I came to admire her. She's overcome incredible odds to get a new business off the ground, to hold her family together through trials and tribulations, and to reach the peak of a sport in which she was initially an outsider. She's been, time and again, a woman in a world made for, and by, men. But she never let her outsider status stop her. Through her faith in God, the support of her family, and her indefatigable work ethic, she became the most unlikely champion. And for me, she became the most unlikely friend.

- *Justin Pahl*, February 9, 2017

Justin Pahl is a writer based in Juneau, Alaska. He grew up in Valparaiso, IN, and attended school in Philadelphia, PA. At the age of 27, he moved to a village on the Greek island of Rhodes, intending to write his first novel. He then spent two-and-a-half years in Istanbul, where he hosted the city's only English-language open-mic night. Over the years he's worked as a gardener, greenskeeper, grant writer, editor, shoe salesman, wallpaper-describer, moon bounce operator, and pizza deliveryman. He's had short stories and poems published and is still working on that first novel.

©Justin Pahl

ABOUT THE AUTHOR

By the age of 70, Vera Koo was both a national and world titleholder in the sport of Action Pistol Shooting. Vera was the first and only woman in the history of the NRA's Bianchi Cup to win eight National Women's titles. She's won two World titles, and was the first woman to place in the overall top 20 at the NRA Bianchi Cup, in 2001.

Born and raised in Hong Kong, Vera's family immigrated to San Francisco when she was 12 years old. She and her husband, Carlos, have a successful business and are the proud parents of three children.

Prior to retiring from sport shooting just 6 months before turning 72, Vera competed in the regular Women's category, as well as the Senior/Super Senior category, in which she competed against only male shooters. As one of the elite female athletes in the growing sport, Vera enjoyed mentoring young shooters as she continued to compete at the highest level. Follow her website, www.verakoo.com, for updates about her career, her blog, and her appearances.

The Most Unlikely Champion is her first book.

ON THE RANGE: APRIL 2013

I've always liked being alone on the shooting range. When I started shooting in my late 40s, I usually shot by myself because I didn't have any opportunities to shoot with other people. Shooters looked at me – a slender, middle-aged, Chinese-American woman – and couldn't believe I was a shooter, too. Maybe they didn't know how to approach me. Whatever the reason, I got used to shooting alone.

After years of shooting on my own, I wouldn't want to change now. I like to stick with what works. Some shooters view range time as an opportunity to socialize. Me? I'm there to focus on my practice. With nothing to distract me, I can achieve that rare form of perfect concentration, the kind that all competitors know well. My solitude is my strength.

I'm a woman who has spent her life in cultures dominated by men. I know talent and luck aren't enough to get what you want in this world. You've got to work harder than everyone else, too. Whenever I feel like quitting, I think back to one of my first shooting mentors, Jim O'Young. If I ever complained or said, "This is hard," Jim would look at me and ask: "Do you want to quit, or do you want to keep going?" And I never quit.

It wasn't at all strange, then, that I was alone at the range on a cold, damp afternoon in mid-April. If most shooters don't like shooting alone, they *really* don't like shooting in the rain. Maybe I don't necessarily like it, either, but I also understand you can't choose the weather. If you plan to be a shooter for a long time, you have to accept that you're going to end up shooting in all kinds of weather. If you're only prepared to shoot in the sun, you're going to have a lot of problems when it rains or gets cold. I once shot in a competition where it was 25 degrees. You have to prepare to be comfortable in any environment. Rain is just another variable a shooter has to prepare for – and if you prepare for it, you can master it.

Normally, I practice shooting near my home in California, but every March, my schedule changes. May is when the Bianchi Cup, one of the NRA's most prestigious action pistol shooting championships, is contested in Columbia, Missouri. As a competition that values precision over speed or flair, it's become my best competition over the years. By 2013, I'd won the Bianchi Cup women's championship a record eight times, including six in a row in the mid-2000s. I was also a two-time women's gold medal winner at the World Championships and had won four team gold medals at the World Action Pistol Championships.

These victories might not have been surprising if I'd grown up around guns, but I'd grown up a traditional Chinese girl in Hong Kong. I was an art major in college and devoted most of my life to being a supportive wife, mother, and business partner. I didn't touch a gun until my 40s and didn't start sport shooting seriously until my life was shaken to its very core. I've probably been the most unlikely pistol champion in America.

Leading up to the 2013 Bianchi Cup, I hadn't been in the right mental place to shoot my best. I was distracted, and my preparation slipped. I don't mean that I hadn't been winning, although I hadn't. To me, competing isn't about beating the other shooters. It's about performing at my absolute best under the circumstances. I hadn't done that during the last few Bianchi Cups. But following a strong run of competitions at the end of 2012, I was confident I would be at my best again for the 2013 Bianchi Cup – even though I was 66, and most of the top female competitors were younger than my daughters.

My longevity in the sport has something to do with the shooter's ability to focus and to tolerate discomfort and hardship. In fact, the best shooters thrive on those things. We're at our happiest when we're pushed beyond our normal comfort zones. Standing in the rain for long hours, your hands aching from firing nearly a thousand rounds a day, isn't what most people would consider fun, but it's when I'm most focused.

Other events in the world also had put my training in perspective. A few days earlier, the Boston Marathon bombing had occurred. The images horrified me, just as the stories of heroism deeply moved me. I couldn't stop reading about the men and women who had rushed to the fore at a time of need to help their fellow citizens. Their heroism was on my mind as I wrapped up my afternoon of shooting. I felt good about my preparations and inspired by my fellow countrymen. This was going to be a better year of competition for me; I could feel it.

As I wrapped up, I moved across the range to throw away one of the targets. This required stepping over a high rope, which marked the boundary between the shooting area and a path leading to the garbage cans. It was the kind of thing I'd done countless times while on the range – dozens of times during this practice trip alone. It was such a simple motion that I don't think I gave it any thought. As a girl, I was shy and petite, but after I married my husband, Carlos, at the age of 23, I'd become quite the athlete. Whether it's snow or water skiing, horseback riding, windsurfing, or sport shooting, I'm always on the move. I never thought that crossing a high rope on the range would change my life.

It was shocking, then, when I felt myself falling forward. Part of my boot caught on the rope. As I hit the cold, wet ground, I felt a searing pain shoot through my right leg.

I wasn't immediately sure I'd broken it. But as I lay there, the pain grew worse, and I knew that whatever the injury was, it was probably bad. I took a deep breath and said a prayer, as I so often do in times of need, before rolling a little to my left to check the damage.

What I saw wasn't good. When I moved my right leg to the left, my foot hung to the right. I knew I'd broken my bone. I could feel the afternoon's chill in my body despite the five layers of clothing I wore. With a broken leg, wet ground, and night falling, I knew I was in trouble.

Being an athlete in a sport where precision and quick decision-making are imperative has worked to my advantage many times, but perhaps never more than lying there on the cold, damp, Missouri ground, my right foot just hanging from my leg. Despite the pain, I didn't panic. I quickly considered my options. I knew my cell phone was in my rented SUV, about 25 yards away. I could yell for help, but the road was at least 75 yards away, and it was made of gravel. On a cold day like this, with a slight drizzle falling, no one would have their windows down. The odds of someone hearing me weren't good, and yelling would just waste precious energy.

I also knew I could stay put, try to conserve energy, and hope someone would find me. This was appealing, as it would allow me to minimize any further damage to my leg. But it seemed unlikely anyone else would come to the range that day, which meant I'd have to spend a night outside in freezing temperatures. I also didn't know if the break had severed any blood vessels. If I was bleeding, I wouldn't make it through the night.

My last option, and the most unpleasant one, was crawling to the parking lot, more than 25 yards away, and somehow mustering the strength to pull myself up into my large SUV. Every movement, no matter how slight, sent searing pain shooting through my leg. The thought of crawling 25 yards was nearly unbearable.

But after a quick deliberation and considering all my options, I knew it was the only choice. No one was going to help me. I would have to save myself.

I needed to move quickly, before the cold and shock set in. But I also needed to mentally prepare myself for the long, painful journey ahead. It's funny how the smallest things can change our perception of the world. Just a minute before, 25 yards had seemed like nothing to me, a distance I could easily cover in mere seconds. Now, all of a sudden, 25 yards seemed like an almost unbearable journey. The world had changed right before my eyes.

I didn't want to crawl, but I had no other choice. Once more, I thought about the recent victims of the Boston Marathon bombing. I told myself that what I was experiencing was nothing compared to what they'd overcome. If they could do it, so could I.

Despite the pain, my thoughts were clear. I prayed constantly. I truly believe that I had help, someone guiding my thoughts and helping me focus. God's presence was with me the entire way. I don't think I could've made such big, quick decisions on my own. For instance, I somehow knew I needed to elevate my broken leg. If I dragged it across the ground, I'd tear more tendons and blood vessels, risking further damage or even infection. But how could I have known this without any medical training and under the stress of that moment? I couldn't have, unless someone was helping me. That someone is the one who is always with you, guiding your thoughts even when you're unaware of it: God.

I took off my raincoat and wrapped it around my leg to provide support. I also discovered that if I lay on my left side and elbow, I could hold my right leg up at a 45-degree angle. My three layers of pants helped support this position. This wouldn't have been possible if I weren't in very good physical shape. Being only four weeks away from the Bianchi Cup meant I was in the best physical shape I'd be in all year.

Bracing myself for the pain, I began to crawl very slowly toward my car. It was immediately clear that I wouldn't complete the journey in one effort. Anytime I moved my leg in any direction, excruciating pain flooded through my whole body. In desperation, I remembered a trick I had used 40 years before, when I was learning to ski. If I looked at the entire downhill in front of me, I would be paralyzed by fear at the steepness ahead. But if I focused on the three feet in front of my skis, where the ground was manageable, the journey became less terrifying.

I looked at the 25 yards ahead of me and broke it into manageable distances. I found three rocks along the way, and those became the stations on my journey. All I have to do is reach that first rock, I told myself. Just get to the first rock. Once I reached it, I took a deep breath and then turned my attention to the second rock. By focusing on the few feet in front of me, I pulled myself to the parking lot.

When I reached my SUV, there was one final problem. My leg was shattered, and although I was in good physical shape, I wasn't sure I had the upper body strength to pull myself up to where my phone sat in the cup holder. Somehow, some way, I lifted myself up and reached into the vehicle. Finally, I called 911. Over the last 20 years, I've become a fiercely independent person, but I have to say, I've never been so relieved to hear someone else's voice.

Once the ambulance arrived, I relaxed a bit and evaluated my situation. I knew none of my family would be able to arrive at the hospital before the next day, so I called a friend to meet me at the hospital. He was a nuclear medicine scientist, and I wanted someone familiar with medicine at my side. I like to be prepared. Then I contacted my daughter, Christina, who also lives in California, and my husband, who was in Denver, Colorado, on a business trip. I asked Carlos to cancel my flight and rental car for the next day. After that, I contacted my hotel in Louisiana, where I was supposed to head the following day for a regional shooting competition, and cancelled that reservation, too.

Perhaps it seems strange that in an emergency I worried about such ordinary, everyday tasks. But during my life in business and during my many years as a shooter, I've learned that preparation is everything. I firmly believe that life is 20 percent what happens and 80 percent how you respond. Life will throw unexpected emergencies your way, and the best way to handle them is how you would handle anything else, be it a delayed flight or a snowstorm. You do what needs to be done. You can't allow outside events to excuse you from not performing your responsibilities.

Once I got everything in order, I reflected on what the injury meant. I wasn't overly emotional, but I also knew it would mean missing the Bianchi Cup, the competition I spend my entire year preparing for. It would be the first one I would miss in 16 years. It was difficult, knowing how much work I'd put into practice, especially because I was shooting at a very high level. But as part of my faith, I put my trust in God. Experience has shown me that He has a plan for my life, even if I might not understand the plan at first. Whatever the reason behind my injury, I needed to view it as an opportunity. I couldn't do that if I pitied myself.

At the hospital, I found out I had a spiral fracture of my right tibia and fibula. The doctors were impressed with how well I was holding up, despite my age. While four very large men on the hospital staff set my leg – this was the most painful part of the night! – one of the doctors actually researched my website. After reading about my shooting career, he told me he had no doubts I'd fully recover. Because I would need surgery to stabilize my leg, he also promised they would insert the smallest metal rod possible. This would promote healing at a faster rate so I could return to shooting as soon as possible.

I immediately knew recovery was going to be a long road. But I also knew I'd recovered from worse. I wanted to begin the process as soon as I could. So although the doctors thought I would want to sleep, they didn't know I adhere to the oldest Chinese healing tradition: eating. *A lot.* I'd just been out in the cold and rain, and I needed to get my strength back any way I could. I wanted dinner.

After eating a big dinner, I settled in. I wanted to sleep, but I was alone in a strange place, and my life had changed in an instant. I tried to stay attentive and be friendly to the hospital staff, but it was difficult. I was worried.

I was surprised when, at 3 a.m., my daughter Christina entered the room. I didn't think anyone would arrive until the next morning. She had a long flight, and the weather was not good. The rain had turned to snow. But there was my eldest daughter, who had flown in and driven two hours on snowy roads through the night to be at my side. It gave me comfort knowing I had raised such a reliable young woman. Finally, I felt safe enough to sleep.

When I woke up the next morning, that moment before I remembered where I was and what had happened was wonderful. Then reality hit me like a ton of bricks. No matter how much trust I put in God, it was impossible not to be disappointed about the injury and missing the Bianchi Cup. I'm an active person, and being confined to bed goes against my nature. But I also knew I had to look forward at the road God had put in front of my feet and not at the road I wished were in front of me. My obstacles and challenges had suddenly changed from shooting at a world-class level to just learning to walk again. I knew I needed to tackle this challenge with the same devotion and seriousness I would've used to tackle any other.

The surgery to install a small metal rod went well, and the doctors told me that my leg, although broken, would heal faster because of the procedure. For many people my age, the procedure would have been impossible. Their bodies would have been too frail to handle it. But the years of looking after my body had paid off. Still, the doctor told me it would be a long road back. I wouldn't be able to touch down with my right foot for six weeks. I'd likely have to use a cane for at least six months. The swelling and pain could last for more than a year.

Hearing this, I immediately promised myself something: I would shoot at the 2014 Bianchi Cup. It was just over a year away, but I would be there. That morning, I started plotting my recovery. I imagined the other shooters standing at the line. I imagined myself standing with them. I knew it wouldn't be easy. In fact, I knew it would be one of the more difficult challenges of my life.

But that was OK. It wouldn't be the first time I'd beaten the odds and overcome something that everyone thought would break me.

THE BEGINNING

haven't always been comfortable with shooting. For much of my life, guns terrified me.

I first went shooting in the 1980s. Carlos had always been active, and he and I had taken up many sports over the years – everything from horseback riding to windsurfing. Carlos is always on the move. I love that about him. He's like a jumping bean when it comes to activities. We'd come home from skiing at midnight, and then he'd drive us to the woods so we could camp.

It was because of those camping trips that Carlos bought a few small pistols to protect us from bears – or so he thought. Little did we know that such small-caliber rounds would have only further angered a bear! But they were Carlos' guns, and I was very uncomfortable around them. He often showed me how to load and unload them, but I could never remember these lessons. In truth, I never handled the guns. They scared me too much.

The first time I handled a gun was when Carlos took me trap shooting. I was such a novice I couldn't even pull the trigger! The range master had to teach me how to load, handle, and shoot the gun. When it came time to shoot at the pigeons, I managed to hit eight out of 25. This might not sound impressive, but considering it was my first time, the range master was impressed. So was I. I'd finally had my first taste of shooting and, although I wasn't yet comfortable, I felt better about the guns.

A few weeks later, I was out to lunch with some female friends. One of them suggested we go shooting in the hills, at the Los Altos range. She thought it would be a fun girls' day. But when we got there, only one out of four of us knew how to handle a weapon.

The moment that convinced me that *not* knowing gun safety could be dangerous came a few weeks later. One of our friends had just bought a .30-06 rifle. He suggested Carlos and I go shooting with him. When we arrived at the range, his rifle sat on a table, pointing down-range. He invited me to fire it. Totally unprepared, I picked the gun up, and it accidentally fired. Thankfully, it was still pointing down-range, but the moment was a shocking wakeup call. I decided that guns themselves weren't dangerous, but my ignorance of them was. I asked the range master if there was some place I could take a firearm safety class. He recommended De Anza College.

Although I wanted to become more comfortable around guns, the decision to take the course was not easy. It was difficult to find time. At this point, in the late 1980s, I was working with Carlos at our family's real estate business. I had a young son and my two older girls at home. It took me a year and a half to make the decision, but I finally signed up for the course, which a cop taught. There were 22 of us in the class, including just three women. I was a good student, always listening, and I showed promise. I hit my first target near the center. From the outset, I was an accurate shooter. After a few classes, I set a goal: I would become the best female shooter in the class.

After three months, I achieved that goal. Despite this, I didn't feel I'd mastered the class. I wasn't completely comfortable with the gun. I asked the instructor if I could retake the course. I had to seek permission, because the college provided students with their guns and ammo for the class. Thankfully, he said yes.

After one more course at the beginner's level, I moved up to the intermediate class. During this course, I decided I wanted to be the best shooter in the class. It was a much bigger goal. Initially, it seemed impossible. Most of the students in the class came from shooting backgrounds. They'd been shooting for years. Some were even private security officers. I was just a mother, wife, and businesswoman. Who would expect me to excel at shooting pistols?

In the advanced class, the instructor would set up targets, and two shooters would come to the line and compete against one another. Whoever hit the necessary targets, in the shortest amount of time, won. To become the best shooter in the class, I knew I needed to practice for many hours so I could harness my emotions and fears in a constructive way.

I wasn't daunted by the task. Goals are important to me. I think of them as seeds. When I decide to plant one, it's going to branch out and germinate in my mind until I see it to completion. Setting goals helps me to keep moving forward in my life. When, after 18 months, I became the best shooter in the class, I knew I needed another goal to keep me going. I was 43, and I vowed to see how far I could make it in the sport shooting world before I hit 50.

Unfortunately, despite the classes I had taken – seven in total, all taught by law enforcement officers – I still didn't know much about guns. At least, I didn't know much about the best guns for shooting. Carlos was still buying my guns for me, and with the classes ending, I wasn't sure how I was going to keep improving.

That's when one of my instructors, Jim Gong, suggested sport shooting competitions. If I really wanted to improve, he said, the best way would be to go out and compete at local club matches.

I wasn't sure I was ready. If I was going to do this, I wanted to do it right. I've always understood that if you want to be good at something, five and 10 are magical numbers. It takes five years to get your foot in the door and 10 years to become truly good. If you want to be better than good, it takes even more time. I knew that if I was going to start competitively sport shooting, I'd want to be better than good. It would mean a long commitment, and I didn't know if I could make that commitment. I had a family and my family's real estate business to worry about. I couldn't just run off and devote myself to shooting and forget about my other responsibilities. That's not who I am. If I was going to shoot competitively, I was going to do it only after I'd fulfilled my responsibilities to my family and work.

I also wanted to make sure I had the discipline and work ethic to succeed. I didn't want to devote myself to something and then not reach my potential. I spent nearly two years studying the competitive sport shooting world before I entered a competition. What I learned was that most serious competitions are a combination of accuracy and speed. I was practicing at the range constantly, and I knew my accuracy was very good. But my speed was a major concern. I needed to improve.

I wasn't trying to reinvent the wheel. I knew that to succeed, I needed someone to show me the ropes in competitive sport shooting.

心平

Normally, a new shooter wouldn't have much trouble finding a mentor. But during those early days, a lot of people at the range didn't take me seriously. They saw me – a petite, middle-aged woman of Chinese descent – and I didn't look like what they thought a shooter looked like. I can't say I blamed them. If you looked at me, you probably wouldn't think I can handle a gun better than most people in the world. In fact, if you looked at me, you might not think much at all.

I was born in Hong Kong, the oldest of three siblings. My parents were what, at the time, would've been middle class. They were both incredibly attractive – more attractive than any of their children. At first glance, they were typical of Chinese couples from that time. My father was a businessman, the right-hand man at a trading company. At home, he projected an aura of stern detachment. He was the head of the household, and my mother respected his position.

My mother kept the home, and she was very dutiful of her place as a woman within traditional Chinese society. She was to fulfill her husband's needs above all else. When she had time, she met with her female friends for tea and shopping. She was expected to present a good household, which she did for events like Chinese New Year, when she woke me and my younger brother and sister at 5 a.m., dressed us in our new clothes, and combed our hair. She gave us tea and sweet candies before preparing to welcome all the well-wishers, who started arriving at 6 a.m.

As I grew older, I learned my mother was a rarity in that era. She'd had a previous marriage, but she'd left her first husband because he was abusive. She'd also left behind two children, a boy and a girl. Although I was the first child between my mother and father, I was my mother's third child.

I was often teased because I didn't look much like my father. My grandparents sometimes teased me by saying, "Your name is not Fang," which was my father's name. I would get angry and shout back, "I am Fang!" At the time, I didn't think anything of these jokes or the fact that I didn't look much like my father. I assumed people were gently making fun of me. But much later all of these jokes would make more sense.

My memories of life in Hong Kong are not very detailed. I remember that period of my life with the broadest brush strokes. I remember my father taking us out on Sundays for afternoon tea and then a movie matinee. I remember sick days, when my mother rented comic books from the shop downstairs and brought them up to me, along with dried plums, which I loved. And I remember I spent a lot of time playing with dolls and looking out from our third-floor apartment window.

Many of the other kids – those whose families had a bit more money – played sports or music or learned ballet, but we weren't quite that well off. I was an avid reader, but my parents didn't expect me to perform well academically. I sort of just coasted through school. Most Chinese parents at the time were very strict when it came to education. They expected their children to bring home straight A's. In this regard, my parents were very different.

In other regards, though, they were very traditional. But, I realize now, they were products of circumstance. My father was often working, and this was to be expected. He rarely engaged with me on a personal level, choosing instead to play the role of detached patriarch. My mother, after bringing the comics and dried plums, would go out with her friends and leave me with the maid. She loved playing mahjong – maybe a little too much. Once in a while, she'd come home so late that the apartment manager would lock her out. My parents occasionally fought about how late she stayed out playing mahjong. To some people, it might seem like they weren't involved as parents. But they behaved normally for Chinese parents of that era.

My mother was the most influential person in my life, which was common for many Chinese girls back then. It was a different time, and parents weren't as open with their children as they are now. Still, over time, I learned some surprising things about my mother. I was not, in fact, my father's child. I was the product of a previous marriage, one I knew nothing about until my mother got dementia and started talking about the man she said was my biological father. But she never told me anything about him, and all I've heard has come secondhand, from my husband.

Chinese women in my mother's time had few opportunities. My mother was bright, a great cook, and extremely charming, but she never had the chance to be anything more than a wife. She was expected to cater to my father's every need without complaint. More than that, she was expected to look the other way when it came to the "other" women in my father's life. I don't mean to speak badly about my father, but it was very common then – it still is – for men from China to do whatever they wanted. It was and is a society that put men's needs first. Wives were expected to not ask questions.

My mother never did. She never complained. No matter what late hours my father kept at the office, no matter how stifled she might have felt about her own limited options, my mother was an eternal optimist. Although she often claimed that life was more hardship than happiness, you wouldn't have known it from her attitude. She taught me that you see the doughnut, not the hole.

My mother was very honest, and in some ways, she favored my younger sister, who was more naturally beautiful than me. She repeatedly told me: "Vera, you are more plain-looking, so you have to develop your inner beauty." Maybe this wasn't the best thing to tell a young girl, but I certainly took the message to heart – in ways both good and bad.

One of the good ways was I knew, from a young age, that I needed to work harder than anyone else. It also meant I got used to being overlooked. It didn't faze me one bit when people took me lightly. It was common. When I started shooting, and the nearly all-male groups at my early competitions didn't take me seriously, you could say it was something my whole life had prepared me for.

心平

My childhood prepared me for a lot of things. When I was 12, my parents relocated our family to San Francisco. They came to the U.S. to give us better opportunities.

But the first years were difficult, as they are for many immigrant families. When we arrived, my father worked as an insurance salesman. Later, once he got his qualifications, he worked as an engineering designer at Pacific Gas and Electric Company, but before he got qualified, my mother worked to help support our family. This was a dramatic change for her after many years of living a comfortable middle-class life in Hong Kong. But she took it in stride. She found a job working as a hostess at a famous Chinese restaurant in Chinatown. She'd go to work looking gorgeous in her traditional Chinese dress.

We lived in a house near San Francisco State University, and I would stay there until I got married. I didn't have much to do in those days except go to school. It was unusual, maybe, for kids of my generation not to have more chores, but I had to walk 27 blocks to school, so that was quite a bit of work!

I remember my mother coming home from work with delicious food – sweet and sour pork, Chinese beef and broccoli. She must have been exhausted from standing on her feet in heels all night. But she was still a devoted wife, and as soon as she got home, she'd start scrubbing the floor and doing laundry. I learned a lot about life from my mother, but above all I think I learned that your first responsibility was to your family. No matter how tired you might be, you still had to do right by them.

WHO IS THAT OLD WOMAN?: APRIL 2013

I woke up in the hospital bed two days after my surgery. The pain wasn't too bad. I'd spent 20 years of my life dealing with extremely grueling physical conditions. Over time, I'd learned that you can think away pain.

What shocked me, however, was when, with the help of a walker, I got to the bathroom. I stood at the sink and looked at myself in the mirror.

Who is that old woman? I wondered. *Whose face is that?*

It was as if I'd aged 15 years in three days. I barely recognized myself.

Lying in bed didn't help. I'm used to being active and running from activity to activity. Being stuck there when all I wanted to do was begin the recovery process made me feel pitiful and pathetic. Here I was, 66 years old, and I couldn't even go to the bathroom on my own. I couldn't even have a shower.

There was one thing I could do, however: eat. Again, this is one of the most tried and true recovery methods in Chinese culture, and for a petite person, I have an enormous appetite. I'd start with huge breakfasts – three pancakes, eggs, and both bacon and sausage for protein. For lunch and dinner, I'd eat huge steaks, potatoes, multiple helpings of veggies – and to top it off, a slice of chocolate cake for dessert.

But eating could only help so much. Lying in bed, unable to do almost anything, it was hard not to have doubts about my future. I could see in Christina's eyes that she wondered if it was a good idea for me to be as active I am. She began to wonder whether it was a good idea for me to be trotting all over the country – the *world* – to compete.

"This is what getting old looks like," she told me.

In one part of my mind, I worried she was right. Maybe my struggles the last few years at the Bianchi Cup weren't just a momentary blip, a brief downturn. Maybe I really was getting too old for this.

After five days in the hospital, I finally checked out. Unfortunately, I still wasn't healthy enough to fly. I would have to stay in Missouri for at least another week. Thankfully, by this time, my husband, Carlos, was with me. He checked us into a room at the Hampton Inn. I would've rather been on our way home, but being out of the hospital meant I could finally, after five days, take a bath. The water hit my hair, and it was one of the great reliefs of my life. The grime finally washed away. For a week I had been reminded how many simple, basic things I took for granted – walking, dressing myself, showering whenever I wanted. Although I was still disappointed about missing the Bianchi Cup, I was already beginning to see that God was sending me a message. I was able to appreciate all the things I'd taken for granted.

And now I wondered: What else was He trying to show me?

Although I couldn't begin rehabbing my leg for another few months, I knew I wanted to get to work immediately. With Carlos' help, I started training in all the ways I could. I taped two three-pound boxes of bullets together and started lifting them, just to keep my muscles used to physical activity. Combined with the enormous meals I ate, I felt stronger by the day.

I grew strong enough to fly back to California after eight days in the Hampton Inn. It wouldn't have been possible had Christina not coordinated almost everything – all the luggage and logistics. Two weeks removed from surgery, the doctors were still worried about the pain and the possibility of blood clots forming when flying. But I'd spent 15 years competing in a sport where you have to block out all external distractions. Pure focus is the goal in sport shooting, and although I haven't mastered it, I've gotten pretty good. With a whole row to myself on the plane, I spread out and simply thought the pain away.

Back in California, I continued what rehabilitation I could do, mostly lifting arm weights and lifting my leg with the cast while lying in bed. It was difficult. After an adulthood on the go, I was effectively stuck in one place. Since I'd gotten serious about sport shooting, it was rare that I took more than a few weeks off. Two weeks without shooting became months, and it shocked my system. It would be like if a writer couldn't write or a singer couldn't sing. Meditation was recommended, but sport shooting *was* my meditation, the place I went to clear my head and block out the world.

I began to doubt myself. Could I really recover in time for next year's Bianchi Cup?

I had experience with such uncertainty. In 1980, when we lived in Singapore, I fractured my spine while horseback riding. It left me laid up in bed, unable to move, for two months. Within days of getting back on my feet, I discovered I couldn't ride anymore. So what did I do instead?

I took up windsurfing.

But I was a young woman then. Now, I was 66.

One of the biggest obstacles I faced in my recovery was that I needed to go prone – to go, as fast as possible, from a standing position to lying down. I shoot in the open category, which means the guns are like race cars – they have a lot of accessories. A race gun weighs about five pounds, including ammo. Open category competitions allow the shooter to go prone and shoot from the ground during two stages of the competition, the steel plates and the practical. In both stages, competitors can go prone at any distance they want. I start going prone at 15 yards in the steel plates and 25 yards in the practical. You shoot from 10, 15, 20, and 25 yards in the steel plates and 10, 15, 25, and 50 in the practical.

Going prone is not an easy or comfortable maneuver, but it gives you added insurance that you'll take the best shot possible. You start in the surrender position – both hands above your shoulders. Upon a visual or audio cue, you draw the gun from your holster, drop to the ground, and shoot from there. Everyone drops to the ground differently. Some are faster, and some go more slowly, to avoid injury.

To compete at my best, I needed to go prone within 200 days of my injury. Yet, day after day passed, and I couldn't even walk. How could I think of competing against the best sport shooters in the world?

Maybe this injury was God telling me it was time to quit.

心平

Despite my concerns, I continued to appreciate many things I'd been too busy or in too much of a hurry to notice before my injury. For starters, sitting in a recliner! When you spend your life running from one activity to the next, you sometimes forget how great it can be to just sit for a few hours. And I was still grateful for every shower I got to take, remembering how badly I had wanted one while stuck in the hospital.

As I slowly relearned things that had once been routine, I was filled with deep gratitude for what the human body is capable of. I'd never imagined dressing yourself could be such a challenge. But I yearned for the days when I would be able to walk easily again.

Carlos made everything possible during my recovery. When I could barely move around the house on my own, he looked out for me. He cooked and bought food, helped set up the shower so I could bathe on my own, and helped me to rehab in what ways I could. Above all, he made sure my spirits never sank too low.

Carlos had been a part of my life for so long that it was possible I didn't see as clearly as I once did how kind and caring he can be. I never take him for granted, but I sometimes forget what a good partner he is. My injury allowed me to see, once again, what a gift Carlos has been to me.

We met when I was 17, the summer after I graduated from high school. I was at a student conference at a resort in Santa Cruz, California, where there was a 10-to-1 guy-to-girl ratio. Most of the guys were graduate students from overseas.

I'd had a relatively protected adolescence, and my father took all of us – my mother and me, as well as my brother and sister – to the summer conference, which the Chinese Student Association hosted. My father's good friend was the organizer.

The conference was one of the first times I socialized with guys. At one point, the camp held a fashion show for all the girls, after which one girl would be named camp queen. This was effectively a meat rack, with all the girls paraded on a runway in their evening gowns. Still, I participated, wearing a long, white, A-line dress I'd made. I had to make all my clothes back then, which I'd learned to do from my mother. With a little bit of campaigning help – also from my mother – I was named the camp's queen, to my great surprise.

I was conscious that a lot of the women there were probably more qualified than me. Many were graduate students, and I thought many of them were prettier than me, too. For many years, I had a deep insecurity about my looks. Part of this, of course, was that my mother always told me I'd have to impress a man with my inner beauty, implying that I didn't have much outer beauty. Maybe that was harsh, and I certainly carried it with me, but in a strange way, I feel part of my ambition stemmed from this insecurity. It took 30 years of hard work to finally grow out of my inferiority complex.

During the student conference, a young, baby-faced man approached me and my best friend. He came over confidently to say hello, which was strange because not only did he look a good two years younger than me, but, because I was wearing heels, he was also shorter than me – and I'm not very tall! His name was Carlos, and he was in a frat. I warned my friend to be careful of him; I'd heard frat guys could be tricky when it came to dating.

That evening, some of the guys at the camp came to our hotel, which was near the main conference center. The guys serenaded us from beneath our windows and invited us to walk on the beach. I didn't go, but my friend did. Before she left, I told her, once more, to be careful.

The following weekend, my mother invited some of the guys from camp over for lunch at our house. Although all the other guys came wearing casual clothes, Carlos showed up wearing a suit – and carrying a cake! He'd obviously come to impress.

I didn't expect to like any of the guys, including Carlos, who was a sophomore at Stanford. But even though he was short and looked so young, I admired his warm eyes and big smile. But he spent the entire afternoon talking to my mother! I couldn't hear what they talked about, but he made her laugh. About the only thing I heard was when my mother said he should ask my younger sister, Sue, out.

After overhearing that part of their conversation, I was surprised when he asked me out instead. I had my doubts about saying yes. He was a fraternity guy, after all. While trying to decide, I remembered a conversation I'd had with my father. He said if you marry a businessman, you'll have money, but you'll never know what time he'll be home. If you marry an engineer, you won't have much money, but you'll know what time he'll be home every night. I'd vowed then to marry an engineer. Carlos was studying electrical engineering.

Plus, he'd brought a cake.

心平

I still remember my first date with Carlos, even though it was nearly 50 years ago. He took me to dinner and afterward he parked his car. He wanted to neck, as they called it then. This was a big step for me. I didn't have much experience dating. Chinese culture at the time was very conservative. There was an expectation that, as a woman, you would only be with one man – the one you married. You would be a loving, devoted wife. The only thing my mother had told me about sex was that a baby came out of the belly button. This made sense to me, because pregnant women's bellies got so big, but you can imagine how embarrassed I was when I told this to friends in high school.

The only dates I'd been on prior to Carlos had been less than a year before, with a guy I'd met in a summer school art class. I ran into this guy when I was at the theater with my mother. He had a reputation for being a bit of a playboy at his college. It made sense. He was the suave and handsome type. He asked me out, but I told him I would have to ask my father for permission. When I asked, Dad said no.

The guy was persistent, though. He kept asking. He insisted that his father had agreed to meet mine and that our date would be chaperoned. Eventually, my father agreed. The "playboy" and his father came over, and then his father dropped us off at the Chinese Association for a dance. The two of us dated for a few months, and his family wanted me to marry him, but I didn't think he would make a stable life-long partner.

I had my concerns about Carlos, too. Although I enjoyed kissing him in his car, I worried that he might not be thinking of me as a serious partner, but as just another girl to fool around with. He was a frat guy, after all! I pushed him away and told him that if necking was all he wanted, he better not come back.

And yet, he did.

Even though Carlos was at Stanford and I was at San Francisco State (I could commute from home), we spent more and more time together. The longer we were together, the more I liked him. I tried to play hard to get, like a lot of people advised me to do, but I couldn't hide my true feelings. Every time I saw Carlos, I broke into this huge grin. On weekends, we went on dates that lasted all day. My father warned me about this, saying that good girls don't stay out too late. I wasn't sure what he meant by that, but one night when Carlos brought me home especially late, Sue, my younger sister, dumped water on his head. I could see my father smiling just inside the window.

Despite my father's advice, Carlos and I became inseparable. It wasn't unusual, during Carlos' junior and senior years at Stanford, for us to see one another seven days a week. Despite spending so much time together, Carlos still coasted by with all A's and B's. He made it seem easy. My grades, however, suffered. But I didn't care. I was in love.

Even though we were young, Carlos sometimes seemed wise beyond his years. He was one of the first people who knew about my deep insecurity regarding my looks. But in true Carlos fashion, he took it in stride.

"Vera," he said, "you've got to build substance. Everyone's looks abandon them eventually."

It was good advice, and it would prove to be true.

This was just one more example of how deep my connection with Carlos was, right from the start. It sometimes felt like we'd known each other for much, much longer. There is an important idea my family sometimes talked about – the Chinese concept of *yuan fen*, which is like fate bringing people together. If you have *yuan fen*, you feel comfortable with a person. You can talk to them, and it's like you've known them forever. If you don't have it, you're uncomfortable with a person.

Carlos and I had *yuan fen*.

Over the years, I sometimes lost sight of this, which happens with every couple, I think. You get so used to the other person that you take them for granted. But as I began my rehabilitation from the broken leg, I was reminded of why I loved Carlos in the first place. Even after 50 years, the *yuan fen* was still there.

RECOVERY: SUMMER 2013

A few months after surgery, I finally began proper rehabilitation on my leg. I was still eating around 6,000 to 7,000 calories a day and lifting arm weights. I'd also made sure to keep handling my guns so that I wouldn't lose the feel. I'd look through my sights and dry fire, drawing the gun out of my hip holster, aligning the sights on the gun and the target, and dropping the hammer. It's a form of prep that shooters do. It wasn't the same as actually shooting, but it helped me make sure that my muscles didn't totally forget what it was like to handle a gun.

Still, I was anxious. Sitting around and waiting is not something that comes naturally to me. I believed this was all part of God's plan, that I was being tested in a way I hadn't been tested in a long time. But I just really wanted to shoot again.

In my time of need, an old friend came through for me – just like he had many times before.

THE RIGHT MENTOR

In 1991, I was a no-name in the sport shooting world. I'd recently decided to begin competing, but I was still finding my way. I wasn't sure how serious my career was going to be.

I had just bought a used steel gun, which is used in Steel Challenge competitions, a type of sport shooting event at which shooters aim at steel targets of different shapes and sizes. I was test firing the new gun at a local range. It was frustrating. There's always an adjustment period with a new gun. It's why you don't use a new gun in a competition. It can jam or misfire; you don't yet know how it feels. But this was more than just getting used to a new gun. I believed the gun I'd bought wasn't accurate enough.

I decided I needed a better piece of equipment. Unhappy, I asked the range owner how I could get a more accurate gun.

The manager kindly told me that perhaps I should ask the most recent A-Class Steel Challenge winner, Jim O'Young, who came to the range every Thursday. He'd be the right guy to help me get a better gun.

It was a Wednesday, so I figured I'd have to come back the following day. But just as I prepared to leave, I turned around, and there was Jim O'Young – a day early! The manager introduced us, and I told Jim about the problems with my gun. Jim is a confident, good-looking Chinese man, and after I finished telling my story, he sternly leveled his eyes at me and asked, dead serious, "Is it the shooter, or the gun?"

To answer that question, he wanted me to meet him at the range the next day. I came with Carlos and the gun in question. Jim asked me to shoot two magazines of ammo. I wasn't nervous, even knowing what an accomplished shooter he was. I felt confident in my abilities and confident that the problem *was* the gun.

I fired 16 shots at a bull's-eye target. Afterward, Jim fired, too. We shot the same as one another, and Jim was convinced that the problem wasn't with the shooter. He agreed to help me get another gun.

I was happy, but I wasn't satisfied. I knew that to become a better shooter, I wouldn't just need good equipment. I needed a good teacher, too. I didn't know the ins and outs of the sport shooting world. I didn't know what competitions were best and which kinds of shooting disciplines would suit my skillset. Who would be a better teacher than one of the best Steel Challenge shooters in America at the time? So, being bold, I asked Jim if he took students. He said he didn't. Undaunted, I asked him if he would allow me to observe the way he practiced and shot. He was OK with this.

After that, I would meet Jim at the range and watch how he shot steel targets. This was an unfamiliar discipline for me, but I couldn't have chosen a better shooter to watch. Jim was a consummate professional. Like many sport shooters, he wasn't enormously outgoing at first and he rarely showed emotion. He was very self-contained.

However, after a few times observing him, Jim felt comfortable enough to ask me to bring along my gun. From then on, Jim became, in an official capacity, one of my teachers.

When he visited me in June 2013, after my accident, we'd long since become friends and peers. Jim knew how much shooting helped to balance me, and he understood how antsy I got when I couldn't shoot. To ease my anxiety, he helped Carlos set up a small air pistol range in our backyard. It wasn't the same as actually competing, but it was something. It at least mimicked the feel of real shooting and kept me from completely losing that sensation.

And just as he had more than 20 years before, Jim O'Young helped put me on the road back to the Bianchi Cup.

Unfortunately, even with my rehab and the air pistol range, the long recovery time was trying my patience. Ever since marrying Carlos, I'm used to always being involved in activities, be it play or work. My impulse was to push forward, but I knew that if I wanted to truly recover, patience was golden. Biding my time was a real challenge. But my whole life has been about getting through challenges. To rise, you must first fall.

FAMILY

Jim O'Young has been a wonderful sport shooting teacher over the years, but I don't think I've ever learned more than I have from Carlos – not necessarily about shooting, but about what it means to live a full, active life and how to take advantage of opportunities when they present themselves.

After dating for four years, Carlos and I had become pretty much inseparable. Many couples have incredibly romantic, staged engagement stories. They go on a big trip or have a fancy dinner. But not us. One day, Carlos simply said, "Vera, we've been together about four years. Don't you think we should get married?"

I did.

On August 23, 1969, Carlos and I were married at the chapel at Stanford University in Palo Alto, California. It was good to finally be married. Although Carlos and my mother were quite close, I'd struggled to connect with his parents. I thought being his wife would help ease these tensions. The truth was, his parents were very traditionally Chinese, just like my family. His father, a pediatrician, had done his post-doc at Harvard, and his mother was a radiologist. They were high achievers and Carlos was their only child; they were deeply protective of him. As a boy, he'd suffered from polio and rheumatic fever. They feared he would struggle with his health for his entire life and they wanted him to marry a strong, sturdy woman who could take care of him and bear many children.

Needless to say, they thought I looked too fragile, too pale and petite. They worried about me having their grandchildren and caring for their only son.

Of course, it had taken me a long time to meet them, and when I finally did, it was by accident. Once, before we were married, Carlos drove us to a park overlooking the ocean. Unexpectedly, we ran into his parents. At the time, I usually wore my hair in a beehive, so I had my hair up in rollers. I also was wearing my mom's big, fuzzy coat, and I wasn't wearing makeup. Even though I was younger than Carlos, in my getup I looked a few years older than him. Looking back, it's a funny image, but at the time I worried I hadn't made a good impression. I wasn't at all prepared for the meeting. Apparently, my fears weren't entirely wrong.

After our marriage, we spent two years living in the dorms at Stanford, while Carlos finished his Master's and Ph.D. degrees. It was difficult, but we were together. After a trip to Singapore, I learned I was pregnant with our eldest daughter, Christina.

I had no idea what pregnancy would be like; my mother hadn't told me. I wasn't working, so whenever I got sick, I was able to lay down on the couch and eat. To stay active, I'd take walks around campus with a friend. Overall, it was a very relaxing pregnancy. When Christina was born, in 1972, Carlos and I were thrilled to be first-time parents.

As I was now the mother of their granddaughter, Carlos' parents had no choice but to accept me as a member of the family. Despite this, my relationship with them remained difficult. They had spent so many years trying to micro-manage Carlos' life that they wanted to do the same with our married life.

Of course, this wasn't that unusual within Chinese culture. In our traditional families, there is no such thing as privacy. The family matters more than the individual. From Carlos' parents' perspective, it was natural to insert themselves into our shared life and to fret about every little thing, like whether I was too skinny or too weak.

When Christina was a baby, my mother proved to be an enormous help. She was a babysitter we could trust, and she often would come over to watch Christina while Carlos and I went out for a quick hike or an afternoon ski. My mother knew how important it was for me to keep Carlos, who couldn't sit still, company.

A little more than a year after Christina was born, I became pregnant again. If my pregnancy with Christina was a dream, then my pregnancy with Shane was a nightmare. I had very bad morning sickness. No matter how much I tried to eat, I just couldn't gain weight. To ease the nausea and vomiting, my doctor recommended a medicine, Bendectin. I only took it for two months, near the end of my pregnancy, and it helped with the illness. I remembered this in case I might need it for a future pregnancy.

Shortly after our second daughter, Shane, was born, Carlos was offered a great job in Manhattan. It promised us a lot of things we lacked – financial security, a place to start our family, and the chance to have some freedom. When Shane was six months old, my mother-in-law went with Carlos to look at houses in New Jersey. At that point, I was used to having other people tell me where I was going to live, so I wasn't too bothered by that. I knew I didn't have a choice anyway. The move east seemed like a blessing. Finally, I would have room to relax, instead of watching every step I made in our home, for fear of upsetting my in-laws.

When we left, it was very hard for Carlos' mother. She'd always had concerns about her husband's health and harbored some dark premonitions that he would die before her. Carlos' father wasn't as worried; he was less prone to such fears.

Unfortunately, Carlos' mother's worries weren't without cause. But it wasn't Carlos or his father who got sick. Less than four months after we settled into our peaceful life in suburban New Jersey, Carlos' mother was diagnosed with lung cancer. Our stuff was packed up and shipped, and we headed back to California to move in with his parents. Right when I was supposed to be taking charge of my own home, I found myself moving in with two people who had never completely liked me.

I tried to have a good attitude about the move, especially because Carlos was very close to his mother. I admired her; she was deeply pragmatic, like myself. I've always explained the difference between her and my mother in this way: Imagine there are five people and four slices of cake. My mother would've not eaten a slice of cake, so there was enough to go around. Carlos' mother would have re-cut the slices to make sure there was enough for everyone. She was strong-willed, but I respected her.

Carlos' father, unfortunately, could be very mean in private. He was one of those men who seems incredibly gregarious and charming in public but is very nasty to those who are closest to him. If he believed that I hadn't greeted him properly in the morning, he would have me sit there and lecture me for three hours afterward. I would be required to write him a note of apology. It was a struggle living with him.

But Carlos' mother's illness seemed to change everything. I softened toward her. She'd always wanted us to have a big family, because she had had a small one. Perhaps it was the sentimentality that her illness inspired, but I thought it might ease her pain if we had another baby. It would show her that we were on our way to the big family she hoped we'd have.

If I had been a little older, a little less naïve, a little wiser, I would have banished this thought as a flight of fancy. Unfortunately, I was young, naïve, and had no wisdom. I'd also forgotten how terrible morning sickness was. So, soon after moving back to California, I was pregnant again.

Although my second pregnancy had been difficult, this one was worse. Our house was full, and because my mother-in-law was undergoing chemo, I was expected to be caretaker for the entire family. Christina was five and Shane was two and a half. As any mother who has had young children knows, kids at those ages are not easy to handle. On top of that, my father-in-law demanded and expected that I cater to his every need. In his view, this was just what women did. I only yielded because my mother had told me, again and again, that family came before anything else in a woman's life. In fact, she called three or four times a day to remind me that I should treat Carlos' parents like my own. "If you love your husband," Mom would say, "You'll treat his parents well."

I saw my mother every two weeks or so. She'd cook me huge meals, because I was battling such awful morning sickness. I went to her place to eat, and she watched the girls while I napped after the meal. Although I no longer complained about my in-laws or talked about how I was treated by my father-in-law, just being with my mother was a nice break from life with Carlos' parents.

Mom and I went shopping a lot, though I didn't have any money. My mother loved walking around the city and looking at clothes, and she always made sure to buy something for Carlos and me. Once, she bought a $500 down jacket for Carlos. I thought it was way too much money to spend, but she always believed in spending money for good quality. She was proven right: Carlos has patched the jacket over the years, and he still has it today, more than 50 years later.

At home, I kept up the house, doing all the cleaning and cooking. This last part was probably the toughest. My mother was a great cook, but it had never interested me. Now, all of a sudden, I was cooking for six, and everyone had different tastes and needs. Some nights, I had to make three or four different meals. Worst of all, neither my mother-in-law nor I could keep the food down for very long, albeit for very different reasons. Between the morning sickness and my stress over living with Carlos' parents, I spent a lot of time throwing up.

Then I remembered how much the drug Bendectin had helped during my pregnancy with Shane. I could barely keep any food down, so I went back to my doctor and was prescribed more Bendectin. The drug was prescribed earlier in this pregnancy, and due to the added stress of living with Carlos' parents I took it for four months. I'd only taken it for two the previous time.

Carlos and I got the ultrasound results during my fourth month of pregnancy. We loved having daughters, but we were overjoyed to find out that this child was a boy. Sons are everything in Chinese culture. They carry on the family name; they can inherit the family business. As happy as we were, we knew Carlos' parents would be even happier. We knew telling them would ease some of his mother's pain during her chemo and might even make his father a little happier, knowing that there was an heir to his family name on the way.

But we didn't tell them out of superstitious fear. Unfortunately, because they didn't know a son was on the way, I couldn't blunt my father-in-law's rages and temper tantrums, which he flew into every few weeks. I never thought to ask Carlos to intervene. How could I ask him to choose sides between his father and his wife? No, I just endured these rages in silence, as I carried a son inside me and yet still kept the house and raised two young daughters.

Things reached a breaking point two months before I was due to give birth. My father-in-law had family visiting: his sister and her husband, who was Singapore's ambassador to Thailand. I ran errands with the girls, and when I came home to make lunch, my father-in-law exploded at me. He thought I had disgraced him in front of his guests by not having lunch ready on time. Like all of his outbursts, it was completely out of line and disrespectful. I knew he expected me to write him a formal letter of apology, but this time, I decided I wasn't going to do it. This time, I was going to take my daughters and leave. I loved Carlos more than anything, but I couldn't raise my children around his father. What awful things would this man teach them?

The next morning, I woke up my aunt-in-law, who was a kind woman I trusted. I told her I was going to leave. She was sympathetic, but she also spoke logically to me. She told me that although she understood how poorly I was treated, if I really wanted to leave, I should wait until the child was born. Where was I going to go while seven months pregnant, with two young girls? How was I going to support them and care for them on my own?

I thought about what she'd said. I was so pregnant I could barely walk. And the girls were at an age when they required almost constant attention. Although I can be decisive, I also like to stop and assess the situation before I make a major decision. What my aunt-in-law told me was right. Where could we go? I thanked her and waddled back to bed.

This marked a turning point in my relationship with my father-in-law. Encouraged by the discussion with my aunt-in-law and feeling empowered by having actually made a decision, I chose not to let his nastiness bother me. I went about my business that morning without paying him any attention. Naturally, this only enraged him further. He skulked around the house, expecting an apology that he wasn't going to get.

Eventually, my father-in-law picked up the phone. At first I didn't know who he was calling, but soon he made it clear that it was my father.

"Your daughter does not know her place," he said, loudly enough I could hear.

I heard yelling on the other end and saw my father-in-law's expression change. He looked stunned. I never found out what my father said, but from that day forward, Carlos' father treated me with far more kindness.

Two months later, when I went into labor, Carlos drove me to the hospital at Stanford. On the way, we discussed the possibility of getting my tubes tied. Although Carlos' mother wanted us to have a large family, Carlos had seen how difficult the last two pregnancies had been for me. He didn't want me to suffer. Ultimately, we chose to wait until after our son was born to make any decisions about future children.

I refocused after our conversation, knowing that labor was, in some ways, the most difficult part of a pregnancy. I remembered what my mother had told me: Don't yell during labor, because it saps your energy. I did as I was taught, and our son, Bryan, was born – a healthy, happy baby boy. I felt I'd fulfilled my role. I had provided the Koo family with a son. There had been generations with only one son in the family. I'd delivered a healthy son, too. Born full term, Bryan had his father's large eyes and large mouth. Like many Asian babies, he was born with a touch of jaundice. This wasn't unusual, though. Both our daughters had been born with it, and it had cleared up in a few weeks.

Except in Bryan's case, it didn't clear up. Not only did the jaundice not go away, but Bryan didn't seem to be developing normally. For the first three months of his life, though his temperament was good, he just wasn't growing.

It had been a stressful pregnancy, and I worried that his lack of growth might be related to my own stress. Once Bryan was born, I gave him my full attention, constantly rocking him and singing to him, hoping my love would be enough to help him grow. My breast milk was plentiful, and I ate massive amounts of food to help facilitate and ensure that.

Unfortunately, no matter how much I held him or sang to him, Bryan showed no signs of improvement. After three months, our doctor said he needed to do a closed biopsy of Bryan's liver. We all hoped this would clear up what was wrong and help us determine why he wasn't growing. Unfortunately, the doctor didn't get a good sample. He wanted to perform another biopsy, but we were concerned about infection. Besides, I wasn't that alarmed. Bryan looked so happy; how could something truly be wrong?

Still, we wanted to take every possible precaution. My father-in-law had been a well-known pediatrician, and he laid out rules we should follow to help Bryan flourish. Although I didn't always agree with my father-in-law, I respected his intelligence and his professional expertise. We washed our hands until they were raw. Christina, who was already in school, wasn't allowed near her brother for fear that she would transmit outside germs.

Despite obeying the rules, things were still hard between Carlos' father and me. When he blamed me for Bryan's struggles, I wasn't surprised. He claimed I was too skinny to support a young child, that I didn't have enough milk for him. This was crazy; if anything, I had way too *much* milk. But I was used to my father-in-law's abuse. By this point, I'd figured out that no matter what I did, it wouldn't be enough for him.

My major concern was Bryan. To make things as safe as possible for him, I moved out of Carlos' parents' main house and into the guesthouse, where Bryan and I lived in a sterile environment. I continued to rock him and sing to him, whispering loving words into his ear. I made sure to take him out into the sun, taking long walks down our driveway or taking him to see the flowers in our garden. I was trying, through the power of a mother's love, to help my son grow.

I thought this initial struggle would just be a small setback. Soon, I thought, Bryan would grow like normal. He'd grow up with two older sisters and two parents who loved to hike and ski. I imagined all the sports he would play with Carlos when he got older. I imagined watching the two of them skiing together, the whole family taking long hikes through the forest.

And Bryan did seem to be getting healthier. He looked bigger than he had before. Our doctor was still concerned, however, and when Bryan turned six months old, we took him in for another biopsy. I wasn't worried. His face had gotten much fuller, making him look even more like his father. This was one last checkup, and then we could get on with our lives – healthy and soon-to-be happy.

心平

The results of the biopsy were shocking. Bryan had severe cirrhosis of the liver, caused by a rare genetic mutation – glycogen storage disease. The reason he looked bigger wasn't because his body was growing like normal; it was because he was full of fluid. Beneath this fluid, he was dangerously skinny and malnourished. There was nothing we could do, the doctor told us. At best, Bryan had six months to live.

I was gutted. My first son was going to be taken from me. There was a gnawing pain inside me. Somehow I knew that this had happened because of the Bendectin I'd taken for my nausea. It was a feeling I couldn't put into words, but it was so deep inside me that I just knew: Taking that drug had led to Bryan's illness.

I tried not to blame myself, but it was difficult. As I always did, I turned to my mother for support. She tried to console me in the traditional Chinese way, saying that this was simply a debt from a past life; that this represented a kind of balance. But I didn't want to hear that. What mother could possibly consider losing her only son a form of balance?

Of course, my mother also offered genuine comfort. She would come over every two weeks and cook enormous bundles of food, which would last our family until her next visit. She often would take Shane, our youngest daughter, and watch over her. She called me three to five times a day, offering what comfort she knew how to offer.

At that time, no one in my family was very religious. I didn't have the kind of understanding I do now of the way God works, how a part of His love for us is that He tests us in ways we can't imagine. Without God in my life, I was just a mother who wanted to make the best of what time Bryan and I had left together. We continued to live in our small, isolated world. I fed him healthy foods while he played with his toys. Despite all that was wrong, his body still functioned like normal; he just couldn't process any nutrients.

Bryan never spoke during his life, but I know that he knew me and he knew I knew him. He communicated through his eyes. We spent many hours looking at one another while I sang and rocked him. It was the hardest thing I've ever done to look into his eyes and see the agony he was going through, to see his pain and know I couldn't fix it. His stomach, unable to process food, would distend and fill with fluid. Every so often, we had to take him to the hospital to get the fluids drained so that his pain wouldn't be too severe.

A parent wants to protect his or her child at all costs, but there was nothing I could do for Bryan except give him all the love I had.

If Bryan's illness was difficult for me, it was difficult for Carlos in a different way. While I got to spend all my time with Bryan, Carlos only got to see our son in rare moments. He had to suffer at a distance, knowing he would never know his first son in the way he had dreamed. He also raised our daughters while I cared for our dying son.

One night, I remember coming outside and finding Carlos kneeling on the patio in the dark. It was obvious that he was praying, but for some reason, at that point in my life, the thought of prayer didn't move me. I didn't fully understand it. Seeing Carlos like that made me realize the agony he was in. I knew I had to be strong. I had to be a rock for our family in the coming months and years.

If Carlos sought help in prayer, I sought strength in routine. I tried to stay busy, both by caring for Bryan and by sewing dresses and clothes for our daughters. If I was constantly moving, I knew there wouldn't be time to think. I've always been this way – still am, in truth – but looking back, I wish I had taken more time to slow down and reflect.

A social worker had been assigned to our family to help us cope with Bryan's illness. She told us that a child's terminal illness often could strain a marriage, but I brushed this suggestion off. We were fighting on the same front, I said. If we were trying to overcome the *same* problem, why would that cause any problems *between* us? Again, in hindsight, now that God has helped me understand the benefits of prayer and quiet reflection, I wish I'd talked about things more. Sometimes, my desire to act can be too quick. I've learned this over the years, and my son, Bryan, helped me. I see now that God used Bryan to teach me this lesson.

Of course, the other reason I disregarded the social worker's advice was because I believed in Carlos. Our relationship was strong, and it would have to stay that way to get us through the loss of Bryan. We'd faced difficulties before. This was another challenge, the most difficult one yet, but I knew we would face it together. This is how it had always been. I knew, in the depths of my soul, that Carlos would always be there to hold me up during difficult times. And, in turn, I would do anything for him.

Shortly before Bryan died, we organized a family photo. The girls wore dresses I had made. They loved Bryan, despite how sickly he was, and treated him like he was just their tiny, cute little brother – which he was. I still have the photo, the only one of all five of us together. Everyone is smiling. We look like a happy family.

Not too many days later, I noticed that Bryan was struggling to breathe. I was only 30. I had no real experience with death. Despite this, as his mother, I knew Bryan was dying.

My mother-in-law came out and panicked. She said we needed to get him to the hospital immediately. If Bryan died at the hospital, there wouldn't be the need for an autopsy. Chinese tradition scorns autopsies – and more than that, my son's poor little body already had endured enough. I didn't want him to be cut open one more time.

While my family prepared to go to the hospital, I held Bryan, rocking him and singing. His breathing slowed and finally stopped. His skin turned blue, and I knew he had died. I wanted to have one last moment with him, as mother and son. He'd been so special to me, and the time we'd shared had been so beautiful, but I knew I would have to let go of him. I just wasn't quite ready to do it.

心平

After Bryan's death, I only broke down once: when Carlos told me he thought I should stay home with our girls while he went to choose our son's casket. The weight of the loss hit me, and I began to cry. I didn't know it was possible to feel a pain so deep and total. It was like a piece of me had been removed.

The day of the funeral, my mother-in-law and I bought yellow roses from Safeway and placed them on Bryan's little white casket. It was a very surreal day. I'd never experienced a funeral before, and my daughters didn't quite understand what was happening. When my parents brought the girls to the funeral, they were skipping around. They thought we were going for a day at the park.

Although my mother-in-law had worried, there was no need for an autopsy. Bryan's body was allowed to rest in peace. During the service, his little casket looked so small, so lonely by itself. Being there was almost an out-of-body experience. I felt like I wasn't fully present. Some part of me couldn't fully be there. I needed to feel separate to survive.

On a bright, sunny fall day, we buried Bryan in Skylawn Memorial Park, near Half Moon Bay. The plot was halfway up the mountain, with a nice view of the valley below. It was beside the plots we'd bought for my parents-in-law, so that he wouldn't be alone. We told our daughters their brother had gone to live in heaven, where he would be healthy, happy, and surrounded by love. And that is exactly what his final resting place feels like.

When I turned around from saying my final goodbye to Bryan, my two daughters ran up to greet me. I saw them smiling in their dresses and I knew, right then, that I needed to be strong for them. I'd lost Bryan, but I still had a family to care for – a husband and two beautiful daughters. As my mother had taught me, it was the mother's responsibility to care for the family. In this time of extraordinary loss, I knew I needed to hold us together.

Thankfully, I had Carlos by my side. We'd always been a partnership, supporting one another and acting as the other's strength. I knew this challenge would test us, but I trusted that, like all challenges, we would get through it together.

We all look for hope in desperate situations. Some people turn to drugs or alcohol, but I've never been a destructive person. I believe in using pain for constructive causes, and even though I was devastated, I knew I needed to stay strong and devote myself to the family I still had. This ability to use loss constructively has been one of the most important things I've learned over the years. It can be easy to surrender to hopelessness, but the mark of true strength is to stand tall against loss and sorrow and to use these things as your motivation to move forward, no matter how hard it might be. Devoting myself to my family and to our work would be the best way to move forward. If I dwelled on what had happened, I might never recover. Worse, my daughters wouldn't have a mother, and my husband wouldn't have a wife. I couldn't fall apart.

RESILIENCE

A lot of people don't like pain. I don't like it either, but as I've gotten older and come to know God and Jesus, I've come to understand that pain has its place in our lives. It's often how God teaches us His most important lessons.

As I was recovering from my leg injury, I thought a lot about the lessons I'd learned from the difficulties in my life. I thought about how I'd recovered from losing Bryan. My injury wasn't the same kind of pain, but the lessons I learned then were still beneficial. To get back to a place of health, I had to stay busy. I had to be patient and strong. So even though I was anxious and in pain, I kept diligently doing all the exercises the doctor recommended. I kept dry firing and using the air pistol range Carlos and Jim O'Young built for me.

But I still couldn't go prone. That was going to be the real test, I knew. Would my leg hold up under the weight of my body? Would I be able to get to the ground in time to shoot? If I couldn't, then all my rehabilitation would be for nothing. And as the summer of 2013 ended, I wasn't close to being able to go prone.

I had to be patient, though. I had to keep working. I had to trust what God – and Bryan – had taught me about resilience.

SHING PING

There is a Chinese word that sounds like "shing ping." It's a concept that means having harmony in your heart. It means you've made peace with everything, and you're not holding onto any old wounds or grudges. It's about finding balance.

I've thought a lot about shing ping since I started sport shooting. When I'm shooting, I know I've achieved shing ping if I completely block out all the other competitors and spectators, when I'm only competing against myself. When I've found shing ping, I'm at peace out there.

Shing ping is a concept that can be applied to all aspects of life. After Bryan died, it took me a long time to find shing ping. Of course, life went on. It had to. Our family was constantly busy. Carlos is always moving, and he wouldn't let life stop. He knew that the way out of grief was to be active. The two of us both believed that for life to go on, we had to keep moving forward.

Adapting to Carlos' hyperactivity was the most difficult part of our early years of marriage. I'd grown up with parents from the old Chinese generation. They devoted their whole day to one thing and one thing only. For instance, if my mother had a party to attend, she would spend all day preparing for it. But Carlos? In the morning, he'd take us hiking; in the afternoon, we'd go swimming; that evening, we'd drive to the mountains so we could ski the next morning. It was non-stop.

Underneath it all, despite the activity, we still struggled to cope with the loss of Bryan. Unfortunately, Carlos' mother wasn't getting any better, either. Trying to handle her illness in the wake of Bryan's death was exhausting for all of us. In some ways, it was like Bryan's life force had helped give her strength. As soon as he passed, her condition deteriorated. She died 18 months later, in another devastating blow to our family. We'd endured two enormous losses in just two years, along with the failed move to the East Coast. It seemed like things couldn't get any worse. Carlos was working hard, and I was trying to raise the girls, but life kept piling on the difficulties. We were reeling.

Having endured all these blows in such a short period, we decided it would be a good time to move again. Carlos had been offered a position in Singapore. It would be a dramatic change, and although we'd be going somewhere that was somewhat familiar – Carlos's uncle and aunt (the same aunt who'd helped me during my struggles with Carlos' father) lived there – it would be new enough to give us a fresh start. We felt it would be a good move at the right time in our lives. Carlos' aunt and uncle had always viewed him as more of a son than a nephew, so we'd be close to supportive, loving family.

In Singapore, we lived a comfortable middle-class life. Carlos worked for an import-export conglomerate. He was the director of their engineering division. While he worked, I raised our daughters. Although aspects of Singapore felt like the Chinese culture of our parents' time – many people viewed idleness as the ultimate goal – Carlos and I made the best of life there. Neither of us could accept being idle, so we found our own activities. Carlos, especially, needed to stay active. He was always going, going, going! He never seemed to rest.

By the time we got to Singapore, I had finally started to match him every step of the way. I still wasn't a natural athlete, but I was there, doing every sport he did, working hard to keep up.

Riding horses was one of the things we found to do. I'd been riding for seven or eight years, and Carlos had been riding since high school. He'd learned while living in Brazil and had continued to ride at Stanford. By the time we arrived in Singapore, we were both experienced riders who felt comfortable on horseback, although I must admit that Carlos tended to charm horses the same way he charmed people. He has a gift with animals and just seems to connect with them. He was a natural equestrian who could do jumps on a horse with so much ease.

Even if I didn't have his animal sense, I was a pretty good rider myself. I rode comfortably on English saddle and had taken many jumping classes. I was easy and confident on a horse. Riding together at the Rotary Club seemed like a good way to keep ourselves busy.

Unfortunately, the run of bad luck and difficulty that had befallen us in the United States followed us to Singapore. One afternoon we were in our jumping class. A lot of the horses at the club had low spirits and weren't very responsive. Carlos and I wanted horses that would respond to our hand on the rein. We both ended up on ex-race horses, but mine had a nasty streak. He kept chomping at his bit and his ears were pinned back, showing that he was not happy. Despite his feisty attitude, I'd ridden him many times without incident.

Unfortunately, on this afternoon, he took off at a full gallop, without warning. I held on and finally calmed him down. Right when I thought things were under control, he took off again, this time taking the bit between his teeth. I lost all control of him. When he suddenly stopped, I launched over his head onto the ground.

The pain was immediate and excruciating. It spread up and down my back. Carlos said I went white as a sheet. But there's one rule in horseback riding: You always get back on the horse immediately after a fall. The instructor told me to do so, and I did. Carlos, however, was having none of it; he'd seen how hard I hit the ground. He insisted I immediately go to a doctor.

The first result was inconclusive, but when Carlos' aunt saw me later that night, she said I needed a second opinion. When I saw the second orthopedist, he told me I couldn't leave the hospital and needed to stay for a week. I had fractured my spine, the front and back of the fourth lumbar, but the fracture hadn't gone completely through. If it had – and it still could, if I moved the wrong way – I would be paralyzed.

It's incredible to think that something as thoughtless as looking over my shoulder could have left me unable to walk, but that's how close I came to my life changing forever. When I reflect on this and consider how much worse the accident could have been, I'm again certain someone was watching over me. As my faith has deepened over the years, I see ever more clearly that the accident was a blessing from God. However, I certainly didn't feel that way at the time. I spent the next two months on bed rest while the fracture healed. Having grown accustomed to being active, this was absolutely excruciating. Of course, it was tremendous practice for the recovery from my broken leg more than 30 years later. At a relatively young age, I was being taught patience – the kind of patience that would be invaluable, both for my recovery from injury and in my life as a competitive sport shooter.

Despite being in bed, the doctor told me there were exercises I could do that would aid in my recovery. It wasn't going to be easy, he said, but if I could carry out this regimen, it would ensure that I recovered well. He assigned me seven exercise routines. I needed to do 15 repetitions of each, three times a day, morning, afternoon, and evening. For two months, I faithfully followed the instructions and did every exercise. By the end of it, Carlos told me my back was as hard as a washboard!

For some people, doing those exercises would've seemed like a chore. But that kind of diligence is second nature to me. I've always tackled what I was supposed to do, no matter what the activity was or whether I enjoyed it or not. This attitude has helped me throughout my life, whether I was cleaning a hundred doors at one of our real estate properties or shooting a thousand rounds in a heavy rain, when everyone else had left the range.

When I finally got out of bed, Carlos surprised me: He'd signed us up for windsurfing lessons! I was a little exasperated. Earlier, I'd told him that I wasn't going to learn another sport. The learning process, for me, was agonizingly difficult and long. I assumed I'd go back to riding.

Carlos said that was fine, but he was going to learn windsurfing anyway. I took a step back and thought hard about it. I'd always been chasing him when it came to sports. When we got together, he was already a very good snow skier and water skier. I started way behind him, so I had to practice a lot just to reach his level. If he started windsurfing, I'd probably have to catch up to him someday. I was tired of playing catch-up. Maybe if we both started at the same time, I'd keep pace with him.

And maybe I was also heeding my mother's advice: to keep my husband company in whatever it is he likes to do.

心平

The first windsurfing lesson was a couple of weeks after I got out of bed. The doctor told me I needed to be careful. He also told me it was possible that, due to the serious injury I'd suffered, my spine might deteriorate earlier in old age. Carlos was concerned about me, but for different reasons: I couldn't swim very well. Despite all the warnings, I was undaunted. Early on a bright morning, I found myself standing on the beach with Carlos, ready to learn.

That first day, all we tried to do was stand on the board, which wasn't even in the water – it was on the sand. Despite being on dry land, I kept falling off. Standing on that board was like trying to stand on a piece of soap. I fell again, and again, and again. Each time – my hands bloodied, my legs bruised – I got back up. And then I fell again.

While my classmates progressed, I lagged behind. It took most of them just a few weeks to become proficient at windsurfing. It took me four months. But I wasn't discouraged. I persevered, fighting through my fear of the water and my frustration at how slowly the various techniques came to me. After a few months of using rental surfboards, Carlos got me a board that was of better quality. It made things slightly easier, but it was still very difficult.

Over the years, I've talked to many female friends about their hobbies. Some of them have had trouble finding hobbies their husbands will support. I've always believed that if they want their husbands to support them, they should look at what their husbands are interested in. If your husband likes boating, why not take boating lessons? Then he'll definitely support you. When I give this advice, my friends inevitably say, "Well, what about passion? I'm not passionate about boating."

But the truth is, we're almost never passionate about things at the beginning. Passion comes later, once you've become good at something. And that usually takes around ten years! That first decade, all you're doing is learning a skill. Anytime you have an opportunity to learn a skill, you should take it, because over time, those skills add up. They help to make you a well-rounded person. If you master a skill, the passion will come later.

I won't say I ever became passionate about windsurfing, but after four months of struggle, I was competent at this new sport. I felt a sense of pride. And I'd learned that perseverance ultimately pays off. *If I can learn to windsurf,* I thought, *I can learn to do anything.*

By this point, we'd become settled in Singapore. Life was calmer all around. We had our activities and a relatively stress-free social life. When I reflect on those days, I think of it as a mostly restful time, especially after everything that had happened in the prior few years. Of course, it wasn't all restful. Carlos worked hard, and every weekend we were busy. But it felt like we had room to breathe on our own after living for so long with Carlos' parents.

At the same time, the economy back in the U.S. was struggling. We'd invested a decent amount in stocks, and with the economy down, our investments lost money. We weren't sure what kind of financial situation we would return to when we returned to America.

There were other trials during those years, too – both the normal, minor trials of raising a young family in the right way, and the bigger stuff, like my riding accident.

One last big moment of trouble happened in 1980. During a visit to the U.S., we took a white water rafting trip down the American River, which runs from California's Sierra Nevada Mountains toward the Sacramento River, in northern California. We were on a six-person raft, and unlike the big rafting trips that happen nowadays, all of us had to paddle. I sat on the side of the raft, behind one of our friends. Our guide was leading his first trip down the river in 12 years, and when our raft hit the first eddy, called "The Meat Grinder," my friend, the guide, and I all fell into the river's raging waters.

Initially, I tried to straighten my legs to keep my nose above the water, but they scraped against the razor-sharp rocks. Desperately, fighting the cold water, I remembered the guide's instructions to tuck my knees into my chest, hold my arms out at my sides, and face downstream. Despite this, I was still being buffeted about, the water constantly above my nose. I remember thinking, "OK, this is it. I'm going to drown." I thought about my life and decided it had been a good one, that I'd used my time well. I was proud of my family, and I worried about what would happen to them once I was gone. I wanted Carlos to re-marry and continue living his life. I knew that my parents, along with his new wife, would help him raise our kids.

Then, suddenly, I was pulled out of the raging waters. The current was so strong, I hadn't seen or heard anyone. But they'd found me. The rest of the trip was uneventful, but what I remember about the American River is that it nearly drowned me.

In some ways, Singapore was like coming out of the fast current of my life. It came after a very difficult stretch for our family, and it was good to have some space to get our breath back. Despite the setbacks, like my back injury, I learned a great deal in Singapore. I learned the patience I would later use while recovering from my leg injury. And through windsurfing, I learned the perseverance and dedication that would help me as a shooter. I couldn't see their importance at the time, but it's clear now that God had a plan for me during our time in Singapore.

This, I've learned, is how many of God's lessons work. They're there for us all the time, but we only see them when we're ready. For instance, I would've never thought there was anything to learn in the tedious back exercises I performed after my horse riding accident. But, 30 years later, those exercises paid dividends. They gave me the patience and discipline to rehab my broken leg. Although I haven't always been ready to see His lessons right away, I now know to trust that everything happens for a reason – and to never stop looking for the answers to God's lessons, even 30 years later.

One of the few problems during our time in Singapore was our social life. It was simultaneously conservative – people were not very active – and liberal. I remember sitting on the beach one afternoon with some of our friends. We were there with a bunch of couples. One woman turned to me and said, "You know, you and Carlos are the only couple I know that doesn't fool around."

Just like in Chinese culture, in Singapore in the late 1970s and early 1980s, it was acceptable – and expected – that men would have affairs. I remember hearing my friend's words and thinking, "Of course we don't. We're happy with each other."

This quirk aside, we were sad to leave Singapore – and especially sad to be leaving Carlos' aunt and uncle, who had been like supportive parents. But we had always planned to return to America. We wanted our girls to grow up there, in the land of opportunity. And after having spent the first decade of our relationship working for other people, Carlos and I were ready to strike out and explore some opportunities on our own.

RETURNING TO AMERICA

When we came back to the U.S. in 1982, we didn't have much. Our family had been wracked by loss, and now Carlos didn't have many great job opportunities, either. We took what little savings we had and bought some apartments in the Bay Area, which we planned to rent out. It probably wasn't the best time to buy; the market was at what was then considered an all-time high. But we didn't feel we had many other good options. Besides, we were told, real estate was always a good investment.

One of the good things about being back in America was being close to my mother again. I'd missed visiting her, spending our afternoons walking, shopping, or seeing a movie.

On one of these afternoons, I asked her how she and my father had met. My mother adored my father, but he'd had a few heart attacks, and his health was starting to fail. We talked about my father a lot in those days, about the old memories Mom had of him. When I asked her how they met, she said he'd come to teach the kids English. I assumed she meant her children with her first husband, the boy and girl she'd left behind, but then my mother said, "The little concubines loved him."

Maybe this should have caught my attention, but she said it in Chinese, and the word didn't really register. I didn't think anything of it.

Shortly after returning to the U.S., we learned I was pregnant with Austin. Although it was an extraordinary blessing, it was not an easy time to have another child. At the time, Christina was 10 and Shane was eight. They were in grade school. Our house was also being renovated so we could eventually provide enough space for our children.

While our house was being worked on, we moved into a two-bedroom apartment. Carlos was doing a lot of traveling to China, so I was often alone with the girls. I'd wake them at 7 a.m. and tell them to get dressed. Then I'd take them to a McDonald's for breakfast and to a doughnut shop to pick up lunch; unfortunately, I was too sick to cook.

I'd pick up the girls from school, and we'd go to a restaurant for dinner. I tried to eat as much as I could, due to my pregnancy, but I couldn't keep much down. At home, I'd help the girls with their homework, and then I'd help Christina give Shane a bath. Once they went to bed, my world was just spinning. I felt overwhelmed and dizzy.

Once, when Carlos was home from working abroad, he said he was going to take us to a nice Chinese restaurant. Unfortunately, I was so sick that even though it was a special occasion and Carlos was just back, as soon as we got home, I went to the bathroom and threw up my dinner. After my experience with Bryan and Bendectin, I wasn't going to take any medicine for the morning sickness: I was just going to endure it.

It was a difficult stretch for us. Because I was too pregnant and sick to cook, we even went to Denny's for Christmas dinner. It was not one of our fanciest holiday dinners.

Despite the difficulties, we were overjoyed to learn we were having another baby boy and new heir to the Koo name. It was bittersweet. We knew how happy it would've made Carlos' mother. And it reminded us of Bryan.

When Austin was born, he was a happy, healthy, intelligent baby. Our family finally felt complete. We had our family, a new home, and a new business. It might not have looked like much to the outside world, but Carlos and I were proud of what we'd built. We assumed things were only going to get better, too.

Unfortunately, when Austin was just three months old, my father's failing heart finally gave out. Before he died, he told my mother that she was the only woman he'd ever loved. This was important to her: Dad was the John Wayne, strong-and-silent type. He'd always been popular with women. When he and Mom got engaged, many of his old girlfriends came to the house and asked why he wasn't marrying them instead. They were educated, beautiful women, and it made my mother proud to know he'd chosen her.

Over the course of their life together, she sacrificed so much for him, but those sacrifices were just expected. It was what Chinese wives did. It was important for her to know he valued her. And he did.

心平

When Austin was two years old, the housing market in California collapsed. If we'd had second thoughts about our investments, this wiped them away. Whether we liked it or not, we were now stuck with our properties. Selling was no longer an option. Our only choice was to buckle down, care for the apartments as best we could, and try to rent them until the market improved.

It was exhausting. Carlos and I worked 18-hour days, doing all we could to get our apartment business off the ground. I remember stamping mailers and creative brochures at 3 a.m. I washed all the apartment doors myself – 120 doors! I also planted all the plants in the complex, which meant I didn't have time to work on my own garden until I got home, usually well after midnight. We had to refinance several times just to survive. In some ways, it was like when we'd first gotten married. We had no extra money, so we scrimped and saved in any way we could.

Strangely, I don't remember this as a bad time. Sure, it was difficult, and it's possible the girls remember it as being worse than I do. But to me, it felt like Carlos and I were once again working and fighting toward the same goal. If I'd been worried about lagging behind him, now I knew we were equals. We were sweating together, trying to get ourselves out of the hole we were in.

We also tried to stay active, despite how hard we were working. We wanted the kids to have a normal childhood. Carlos especially wanted the girls to be exposed to things at a young age, so that they would be cultured, experienced women. This meant that we still hiked and skied whenever we could, even if we were utterly exhausted or had barely slept.

Some people might have been discouraged, having to work 18-hour days and clean apartments just to survive. But I often thought back to where I'd started from in this country, when my father brought us over from Hong Kong. We'd had absolutely nothing. Now I had a family, and we owned apartment buildings. That was remarkable to me. This country could take you in, and you could turn nothing into something just through hard work. I've always believed – and always told my children – that if you work hard in America, anything is possible. My life is proof of that. It was never easy, but the American dream wasn't meant to be easy. Even during those long, exhausting days, I was grateful for the opportunities America had given me. They're opportunities I wouldn't have had anywhere else.

Carlos and I worked hard during those years, but we were also the beneficiaries of generosity. Carlos' father, who had lorded over us for so long, had become softer since the death of his wife. Although he was a strict man, I think he was also incredibly lonely and insecure. He just didn't know how to connect with people, and it made his life very hard. After we returned from Singapore, he moved to San Francisco and, in an act of extraordinary generosity, signed over his house to us. This was an incredible relief, as it meant no matter how bad things got, I could look my children in the eyes and tell them we would always have a roof over our heads.

That house was about the only thing that went right for us, financially-speaking, during those years. Sometimes I wasn't sure how we were going to survive. But although I didn't know *how*, I knew we *would* make it through. I remember telling Carlos that we had to treat a dead horse like it was still alive. We would fight to the end; we'd make the banks come and actually foreclose on our properties, including our home, before we ever stopped fighting. And even then, we'd continue to fight. We let our children know that giving up was not something our family would ever do.

And we never did. We survived the turmoil. We fought, and fought, and after seven years, things started to improve. The economy got better, and our hard work began paying off. After many years, we were finally in a position to hire more people to do the jobs that we'd been doing ourselves. With our girls getting older, we were making enough to breathe again.

MODEST GOALS

People sometimes think I began sport shooting with the intention of becoming a champion. It was just the opposite. I never intended to be a champion. I always had very modest goals, and my career built somewhat unexpectedly as I continued to meet one modest goal after the other. When Jim O'Young and I began training together in 1991, I was still only shooting in local competitions, but I was spending more and more time at the range, practicing.

Initially, my family didn't take my new hobby very seriously. Carlos was supportive and helped me pick out the best guns to shoot with, but our kids mostly thought it was humorous. They rolled their eyes at me.

Still, sport shooting was important for me. It gave me a sense of purpose I'd never had before. All the work I'd done had been in service of the family or the family business, and while my family always will be a source of incredible pride to me, I still felt like I'd never had the opportunity to see how far I could take something on my own.

After I finished my first firearm safety class at De Anza College, I talked to Carlos. One of the problems most shooters have, the instructor said, is flinching. You anticipate the shot, and then the noise of the shot causes you to flinch. To compensate for this, you push the gun down, bracing for the recoil. Carlos heard about the flinching problem and went out and got me the .357 and .44 Magnum. He thought these guns would help me to not flinch when shooting in single action mode, which is cocking the hammer before pulling the trigger to shoot.

I don't know why Carlos thought that shooting bigger caliber guns first would guarantee no problems with flinching when shooting a smaller caliber, like the .38 special. If you struggle with flinching, you likely will struggle regardless of the caliber. Maybe Carlos thought this because *Dirty Harry* was in theaters at the time. We'd seen the movie a bunch, and Carlos loved it when Harry pulled out his huge .44 Magnum. In the movie, there was never any recoil, and he always hit the bad guys. In truth, no one would conceal carry a gun that size. I also think Carlos enjoyed the big guns because they impressed some of his business associates. Either way, I didn't have flinching problems. I've never had them, and I didn't use the magnums much.

At that time, I was mostly shooting with a .38 revolver or a .38 semi-automatic. I began going to a range in Milpitas, where they had bull's-eye competitions every week. I still had responsibilities, both at the office and at home – Shane was in high school and Austin, who was born in 1983, was nine years younger – but I managed to get to the range twice a week, including competitions. These were very competitive matches and helped me greatly as a shooter. Some really good shooters competed at the local clubs, and they took their sport seriously. I wouldn't have improved if it weren't for the lessons I learned in these early days.

The most important was that in order to shoot my best, I couldn't pay attention to the other shooters. I couldn't worry about what they did. I just had to focus on my sight alignment on the gun. If I lost my focus at all, if I paused to think about what the other competitor was shooting even for a split second, it could be devastating to my performance. I realized very early on that although sport shooting is a competitive sport, the person you're competing against is yourself. It's about controlling your nerves and getting into a zone of total concentration.

After winning the highest honor in Milpitas, I found another gun club where I could further test my skills. In San Jose, there was a PPC shooting match, which required using a holster. This was a new challenge for me, as I didn't know how to shoot from a holster. I would eventually win three trophies in my final match at the club. The biggest was a massive trophy, given to the first woman to shoot a perfect score, a 600. That had never been done at this club.

Claiming that big trophy became my goal.

It took a long time and a lot of persistence. Just as it took a long time to learn how to windsurf, I found that no matter how much I practiced, I couldn't quite shoot a perfect score. I'd shoot a 596, 597, 598. This went on for a year and a half. Others might have been discouraged or decided that shooting a 598 was good enough and moved on. But when I set a goal, I don't believe in doing a "good enough" job; I believe in completing the job you set out to do.

After many close calls, in 1991, I finally got my 600. I showed up to the ceremony decked out in a dress and high heels. I wanted to accept the trophy as a woman.

At the time, not many women competed in sport shooting. It was definitely another man's world I'd wandered into. A lot of the women who competed did so because of their husbands or friends, or to meet men. At first, it was difficult to dispel the idea that I was shooting to meet a man. This was ridiculous, of course. I was happily married. But in those days, when men saw a woman at the range, they assumed she was there for reasons other than the competition.

In some strange way, I wasn't uncomfortable with this. My whole life had prepared me to exist as a woman in a man's world. Almost every culture I'd experienced was dominated by men – from China to sports to real estate. I'd learned how to navigate these cultures without letting unwanted attention, or the attitudes of those who didn't believe in me, hold me back. I'd developed a very tough skin.

However, this inherent bias made finding a mentor difficult. I've always believed that to properly learn a new skill, you have to learn from the best teachers you can find. With so few women in the sport, I knew that if I chose the wrong mentor, it might raise eyebrows. People might get the wrong idea.

Jim O'Young ended up being the perfect mentor. His sense of professionalism was, and remains, unparalleled. I modeled myself after him, studying his techniques and his practice habits. I also studied how intensely he focused on the task. Like me, he wasn't at the range to make friends. He was there to do his best. Because we are so similar, it wasn't hard for Jim and I to become friends. But we've always remained work friends, in a way. We rarely discuss anything other than shooting.

After shooting my 600, I was training with Jim, who at the time was one of the best Steel Challenge shooters in the world. Steel Challenges, as competitions, require a good balance between accuracy and speed. Shooters take aim at metal targets ranging in size from 10-inch round plates to 18-by-24 inch rectangular plates, which the shooter tries to hit from different distances, between 7 and 35 yards. Because the plates make a loud ping when you hit them, Steel Challenges are great spectator competitions. Jim was so good at that kind of competition, and it made sense that he would train me to eventually compete in the Challenges.

To properly prepare, I needed to find a range with enough outdoor space to accommodate the setup of a Steel Challenge. It needed to be out in the open – outside the city, that is. In my early days of sport shooting, I could just find a normal range with a simple bull's-eye target. Sometimes, I even set up cans in our backyard and practiced with a BB gun. This was great practice, and it helped teach me to feel comfortable with a gun. But a Steel Challenge was different.

Shane and Christina were out of the house by then, but Austin was still in elementary school. After losing Bryan and Carlos' mother, and then living in Singapore, Carlos and I weren't sure we were going to have another son. So Austin was a surprising gift to us. He's always been clever – sometimes too clever for his own good. Because he was the baby of the family, we spoiled him a bit.

Every day, I took him to school and then drove to a friend's ranch in Gilroy, which was way out in the hills. There, outside the city, I practiced shooting Steel Challenge for hours. It was a three-hour drive round-trip, so if I left right after dropping Austin off, I could get a good day of practice in before returning to pick him up.

The ranch was beautiful. Set in the hills, it was surrounded by nature. I shot beneath the vast blue sky. The ranch was owned by an acquaintance generous enough to let me set up my metal targets on her land. After I finished practicing, while I cleaned up and prepared to go home, I often looked around at how beautiful the scenery was – the green of the trees and the deep blue of the sky. It was very peaceful.

Of course, peace on the surface can often mask turbulence just out of view. In the future, I knew I would face some difficult decisions about sport shooting. At this moment, I hadn't been terribly aggressive in pursuing my shooting. I was practicing and going to local matches, but it wasn't a full-fledged pursuit of my sport. I'd won local club matches, but if you looked at me then, you wouldn't have thought I was someday going to become a world and national champion.

My family and friends were among the people who didn't take my shooting seriously. My family thought it was something strange that I did in my spare time, and my friends thought it was a passing phase, just another hobby like horseback riding or windsurfing.

Who can blame them? I didn't know how serious I wanted to be about sport shooting. Yes, I showed promise and had won some regional club matches. Yes, I was continuing to set goals. But I was still a mother and wife first. Between Austin and the family business, did I really have the time, money, and commitment to see how far I could take the sport?

Until that point, I'd spent my life devoted to others – Carlos, my family, our business. This was how I'd been raised to behave as a Chinese-American woman. By the time I was training for Steel Challenges on the ranch at Gilroy, in 1991, I was no longer cleaning 120 doors and floors and planting flowers at the apartment complex during the night. For the first time in my life, I felt like there was enough space to pursue something that was truly, uniquely mine.

I was excited by the possibilities sport shooting provided. Practicing every day on the beautiful range in the hills, I breathed in the clean air and felt like my life had come through the rapids, just like I did all those years ago during our rafting trip. Life, it seemed, was good. Our family was happy and healthy. Our business was going well. I was getting stronger and stronger as a shooter, and I was curious to see how much further I could take my growing skills.

BABY STEPS: AUTUMN 2013

W hen I first broke my leg, my doctor told me that, ideally, there would be a three-month progression. I'd go from a wheelchair to a walker to a cane, and then be able to walk without a boot. In my mind, those three months were how I marked my progress. I knew that if I wanted to shoot at the 2014 Bianchi Cup, I needed to be walking on my own within three months.

In addition, I set a concrete goal. There was a conference, six months after my injury, in Asheville, North Carolina. It was the NRA's Women's Leadership Forum. I'd never been able to attend, because it takes place during my shooting season. November is when the World Championships were held, and I've been honored to represent the United States many times at the event. But due to my injury, 2013 would be the year I could attend the Women's Leadership Forum. I planned to walk in under my own power, wearing high heels for the plush functions. Considering I couldn't even walk when I set this goal, it was going to be a tall order.

I did my sets of physical therapy faithfully, and kept up the exercises that I needed to do for my shooting – using the air gun range Carlos and Jim O'Young had set up for me, and continuing to handle my guns, so as not to lose muscle memory. I also kept lifting weights to keep my arms strong.

Once I moved from the wheelchair to the walker, I'd walk around my backyard. After a bit, I started pushing the walker a few steps away, so I could re-learn how to walk on my own. Once I reached my walker, I'd push it away again – a few steps further this time. Thanks to this, once I left the walker behind, I never used the cane.

Of course, you walk differently in a boot than without. So after losing the boot, I had to rebuild the old muscles.

I was dogged in my rehabilitation, not letting anything discourage me. I knew that progress wasn't going to be linear. My whole life had taught me that. I had to take the downs with the ups and keep looking at the long view. There would be bad days, maybe even bad weeks, but as long as I was moving forward … well, that was what mattered.

This attitude kept with my personality. I've always stared down challenges and known that I'd get through them. My abilities to be patient and persistent have been my greatest assets.

Carlos has often wondered where I got my fierce personality. The father who raised me was a gentle man, and my mother, though a wonderful woman, was not fierce. The answer, Carlos suspected, might lay with my mysterious birth father. Whoever he was, he must have been strong, because over the course of my life, I've had to pull myself up plenty of times. The broken leg was proving to be difficult, but the truth was, I'd survived worse – much worse.

A DEVASTATING DISCOVERY

When I was nine or 10 and my family was still in Hong Kong, my mother would occasionally have friends over for lunches and tea.

I remember one afternoon in particular. All the women who came over were very elegant and stylish. They wore beautiful clothes and lots of makeup. They gave off the appearance of being the wives of successful men.

Except one of them, I found out, wasn't a wife at all. She was a mistress. It seemed strange to me. She didn't look any different from the wives. She was just as well dressed, just as stylish. She looked like any of the wives. And yet, she wasn't.

In that moment, I think a seed was planted in my brain. I promised myself: *I will marry a man who will never keep a mistress.*

心平

In the spring of 1993, our house was much quieter. Our two daughters were off to college. Carlos and I were both extremely proud of them and their achievements. We'd raised two independent, intelligent women, and now they were out in the world, getting an education that would open opportunities that hadn't been available to me – or even to their father.

Despite only Austin remaining in the house, my life was anything but quiet. I was shooting more and more, training with both Jim O'Young and on my own. After dropping Austin off at school, most days I'd drive an hour and a half to the Gilroy ranch, where I could shoot from 45 yards – such a long distance that the ranch was the only place I'd found to accommodate my training.

I took Highway 101 out to the ranch. One day, as I was driving, I looked at everything around me and marveled at my life and the world: the blue sky, the hills, and the freeway surrounded by vivid green trees. It was so brilliant! I couldn't believe how beautiful it all was. Carlos and I had finally emerged from the stormy years, when we were working so hard just to survive. Now the two of us seemed to be doing better than ever. Not only were we financially secure, but Carlos was putting more effort into our relationship than he had in years. When he was in town, he would take me out for coffee about four nights a week. We would talk for hours. It was special to still feel such *yuan fen* after all our years together.

We didn't go for coffee every week, because Carlos was often traveling for work. Our real estate business had improved, but both Carlos and I wanted to make sure that we didn't rest while things were going well. We knew there could always be another downturn, and we wanted to ensure that we'd never have to work so hard again just to survive. We didn't want to have all our eggs in one basket, either, so I encouraged Carlos to invest our money in other areas. This meant Carlos often had to take business trips to China. These were the early years, after China had just opened its doors to outside business interests. Carlos was always on the lookout for new investment opportunities, ways to keep us moving forward. He had impeccable business instincts, and he is the ultimate people person.

I occasionally went on these business trips to support Carlos. The meetings in China always reminded me what a man's world the culture still was. Things were much as I remembered them from my childhood. Women were treated as second-class citizens or objects for men's delight. At dinners or banquets, beautiful young women with smooth faces and big eyes would fawn over the businessmen. These business trips always felt like being let into a "boy's club."

Some of my girlfriends had gone along on these trips, too. They said that some of the men behaved like kids in a candy shop. I didn't worry, though. I was confident Carlos and I were above that kind of nonsense.

In April, I had just returned from China, having traveled with Carlos for the special opening of a joint venture. Our eldest daughter, Christina, had come along, too. The two of us returned a bit early, while Carlos stayed to do some more business.

Christina always liked to tell me that she was our "easy" child: She was incredibly hardworking, had her father's business sensibilities, and almost never fought with either of us. Christina and I spent those first evenings back in the U.S. watching movies and talking. The two of us could – and still can – talk for three or four hours at a time.

On one of these evenings, it was unexpectedly cold for April. We were settling in to watch another movie, and I went to turn on the furnace in Carlos's office. Turning the heating on was always an adventure. Carlos's office was like a disaster zone. You'd think a bomb had gone off in there. Although I'm very organized, Carlos is messy, because he's always running and working so hard. This is in keeping with his relatively free spirit. He's not good at letting go of things, so his office has always been crowded with papers and photos. They're usually strewn all over the place, like they were on this evening.

I turned on the heat, but I was worried about all the paper on the hot vent. While I was moving papers, I noticed that a few things were stuck in the vent. When I pulled them out, I saw that they were photo negatives. I held them up to the light, trying to see what was on them. All I could make out was a series of photos of a girl at a place that looked like Disneyland. There was also a single photo of man and a woman together. The man, I assumed was Carlos, and I thought the girl was Christina. But I couldn't tell for sure.

The next day, Austin had a birthday party to attend. After dropping him off, I stopped by a Safeway one-hour photo shop and got the negatives developed. When they came out, I was shocked: The man in the photo *was* my husband, but the woman was not Christina. It was a young woman I had never seen before. They were at a restaurant, a place Carlos and I had just been with our family. They were very clearly "together."

I couldn't stop looking at the photo. As I stared at it, I started to shake uncontrollably. I felt like my legs had been cut out from beneath me. Who was the woman, and what was she doing with my husband?

I asked the mother of Austin's friend if she would take him home, as I was too stunned to drive any more than I needed to. I went home, but once there, I found myself unsure of what to do next. I had urgent questions, and I wanted answers. But Carlos was still in China, and I couldn't get in touch with him. There was nothing I could do but wait.

I remembered a conversation I'd had just two weeks earlier at a ladies' luncheon. I was sitting with a casual acquaintance of mine. She was very stylish and astute. She looked around the room and said, "The husbands of 75 percent of these women have extramarital affairs." I'd smiled, thinking I was in the 25 percent.

Now? My heart was sinking and I felt like I was fighting for air. How could Carlos possibly be like one of those other men? I believed that the women they cheated with were the young Chinese girls who would show up at business gatherings to entertain the men. These girls were desperate. Although the new "open door" policy had created opportunities for Chinese people, most of the women still didn't have many options. There were almost no opportunities for all the women who wanted a good education. The only way out for most of them was to attach themselves to a man with money, which would hopefully get them to America or Europe.

Had one of these women attached herself to my husband?

心平

I finally reached Carlos in China. I told him I needed him to come home early. I said I'd been to the doctor and had gotten lab results back; we needed to talk about them. Carlos later told me he was so worried he didn't eat or even move in his seat on the entire fourteen-hour flight home. He thought about his mother, who had died from cancer. He was worried that he'd lost her, and now he might lose me, too. Of course, that was a possibility, but not in the way he thought.

I picked him up from the airport dressed in my finest clothes. I looked as nice as I've ever looked. While meeting him at the airport and then driving him home, I managed to stay calm. I still didn't tell him the real reason why I'd wanted him home so soon.

When we reached our house, I showed him the two photos. At first, he claimed it was nothing. But I could see how shaken he was. I pushed the issue, certain he wasn't telling me the truth. Carlos doesn't like confrontation and does everything he can to avoid it. No matter how much I pushed, he wouldn't give me the full details. I asked if she was a stewardess on one of his flights, and he vaguely said yes. That was all I could get out of him.

I'd had trouble sleeping since I'd discovered the photos. I'd actually gotten in touch with my brother, a doctor, to see if he could prescribe me sleeping pills. He refused, but I found that taking Nyquil allowed me to get a few hours of sleep a night. That night, with Carlos safely home, I took some more Nyquil and drifted into an uneasy sleep.

In the first days after finding out what had happened, I tried to hold myself together and keep up appearances. Austin was still in school, after all. And Carlos and I still had a business to run. We had family, social responsibilities, and friends.

But I think I was in shock. My life had been completely shaken, and I couldn't adjust to everything all at once. I was walking around as if life was normal, but inside, I was dying.

Shortly after I found out about the other woman, Carlos and I went on a spa weekend, hoping it would help us begin the process of moving forward – at least, that's what Carlos hoped. But while we were there, it was like I came out of the shock. I saw with clarity how deeply Carlos had betrayed me and how much he had damaged our marriage. I suffered what a lot of people probably would call a breakdown. It felt like I'd had my arms and legs cut off. The spa had to call in their therapist, which ended up being a blessing in disguise – she would be my therapist for the next two years, as I began to rebuild my life.

Carlos couldn't understand why I was so deeply shaken. He didn't know I was going to be as deeply hurt as I was. He just didn't get it; we're different in this way. He thought: The other guys do it; her father did it; this is normal. Shortly after I found out what happened, he told me that I shouldn't take it personally. At the time, I couldn't understand what that meant. I couldn't believe he would say that. To me, love is everything. When I love, I love completely, with total loyalty and trust. The thought of hurting Carlos, or anyone I love, makes *me* hurt. So how could he do something like that? What gave him the right to cut my legs out from beneath me?

I didn't see how I could ever forgive Carlos. I didn't see how the love would ever come back. At that time, the love was gone. I was completely numb. Day to day, I kept going through the motions of my life, but it didn't mean anything. I still went sport shooting occasionally, and I still went to ladies' lunches, but I was dead inside. In photos from this time, my eyes look hollow.

My mind couldn't rest. It kept going over the hurt and how impossible it seemed to fix it. What gave Carlos that right? How could someone do that to another person? I'd always done everything for love and for my family, and here I was, shattered and dying inside. And all Carlos could say was: Don't take it personally.

心平

In May 1993, two weeks after I found out about the affair, I was driving along the same freeway to the Gilroy ranch. Just a month before, everything had been so brilliant and vivid. This time, I looked out the window and it seemed like a wasteland, everything gray and dead. It was as if a nuclear bomb had gone off.

But that was impossible, I realized. It was spring, so how could the world around me be a wasteland? It couldn't be. The wasteland was in my head. And if it was in my head, I could control it. If everything really were dead, it would be outside my control. But this? I could fix it.

The only question was: How?

Considering what had happened, and considering how hurt I was, I seriously debated a divorce. I thought it might be the best way to move on. After all, how could I ever forget what had happened? How could I ever forgive Carlos and look at him the same way again? I didn't think I could.

Not long after driving down that freeway, I got lunch with a friend. At this point, I was just trying to survive minute to minute. All I could do was put one foot in front of the other. I thought seeing a friend would help me to survive those few hours. Instead, it made things worse. I told her what had happened, and her response floored me.

"Well, a lot of women like Carlos," she said. "He's fun. Even I like Carlos!"

I couldn't believe it! This was the last thing I needed to hear. I'd spent years building my relationship with Carlos, working at things I wasn't naturally good at, and here was this friend implying that what had happened was somehow natural.

I left the meal convinced I needed a divorce. I could never get past what had happened.

Afterward, I had to pick up Austin from school. On the way home, we went to the grocery store to get food for dinner. He said he wanted to cook for me. I was still very upset from lunch, but I remember coming into the kitchen at home and seeing Austin cooking. He was barely tall enough to reach the counter, his head just peeking over the top. He had one blue sock rolled halfway down his ankle. I looked at him and thought: I need to finish my job as his mother. I need to finish the job, for him.

That day sort of summed up what those first months were like: a constant struggle between thinking I couldn't possibly fix the marriage, and moments of realizing that I needed to fight on. Specifically, there were two more times when I absolutely thought that I was going to get a divorce.

The first came after I went to our vacation house to be alone. I told Carlos where I was going and said I needed some time on my own to think.

While I was there, Carlos called me. The two of us talked for three hours. It was a brief reminder of what we'd once had – all the capital we'd built over 28 years of marriage. It made me feel better, and, even though it was the middle of the night, I decided to go home.

I drove home and arrived at 3 a.m. But when I got there, I found our bedroom empty. I lay in our bed, waiting, but Carlos didn't come in until 5 a.m. He'd been seeing her. It was honestly like feeling my heart break on the spot. To have that happen after the conversation we'd had? I couldn't believe it.

After that, Carlos went to sleep in the guest house, where we'd lived during our time with my in-laws. While he was there, he spent the whole two days sleeping on the mat by the door. I saw how much of a toll it took on him. I almost understood. Carlos is a gentle soul; he wasn't just going to be able to cut this girl off and drop her like nothing. It's not who he is. But then, what about me? Why wasn't he worried about how this affected me?

Still, I felt bad enough that I let him back in. But then I asked him if he loved her. If this was love, I could understand it. Yes, it would hurt, but love I understand. I wasn't going to get in the way of love.

He said he didn't love her.

I told him then that I would give him time to end it – but that he better not take too long.

心平

Those first months were some of the hardest of my life. Losing Bryan had been devastating, but at least in that loss, Carlos and I were fighting together for the same thing. Our path forward was clear. We had no choice but to move on with our lives, caring for our daughters as best we could and going ahead with our business. We were on the same team, working toward the same goals. But now? I didn't know which way to go. There was no direction that made sense. There was no plan. And instead of fighting together, we were fighting each other.

I was desperate for help, but I didn't know where to turn. Some friends advised me to stay with Carlos. Everyone liked him. Even my brother said, "If it was anyone else, I'd say leave. But I like Carlos."

I was dying inside. In those moments, when I didn't know how I'd survive, I began thinking more about prayer. I didn't know much about prayer or Jesus. My family had never been religious. Carlos, in particular, has never had any sort of religious beliefs. We had never really practiced any faith as a family.

A friend of mine, Rose Jean Fong, was a very devout Christian. Over the years, Rose and I would see one another at various ladies' luncheons, where we'd talk. After one of these talks, she started sending me Christian pamphlets – they were called *Guideposts*. Many of them talked about prayer and how God hears our prayers.

I never understood why Jean started sending me these, but when I hit a point where I didn't know how I was going to survive, I thought about the pamphlets and decided to give prayer a try. I would kneel down and talk to God. Within the hour, some small, good thing would happen to help me survive. When you're struggling to take your next breath, something as simple as a nice smile from a stranger can help you survive.

With my life so shaken, I was struggling to focus on my shooting. I couldn't clear my head or stop thinking about Carlos. I was still going to the range once or twice a week, but I wasn't progressing. Though Jim O'Young was still calling me to go and compete in Steel Challenge matches in Southern California, I wasn't taking him up on these offers. It seemed possible that my career as a shooter might be over before it really began.

I turned everywhere I could for help. I talked to my mother constantly, and she thought it would be a good idea to visit one of the best fortune-tellers in the city. I appreciated Mom's concern, but it didn't help me to see a better future.

I tried more traditional means of therapy, too, meeting with an intuitive counselor, as well as my therapist. Again, I believe in the Chinese idea of "shing ping," which means that if you're harmonious with yourself, you'll be harmonious with the universe, too. I definitely wasn't harmonious with myself. The question I kept asking was: With Carlos still in my life, how would I ever reach that state of harmony again? Would I ever look at him and see anything other than how he'd hurt me?

During this turbulent time, I talked a lot to my best friend Cecilia. She was sort of "keeping an eye on me." I could call my therapist on an emergency basis, but Cecilia was a constant. She's an incredibly bright, wise person, who sees things very analytically. I trust her completely. I knew that whenever I needed to talk to someone, I could call her, and she would listen and offer advice.

Despite Cecilia's support, there were moments when I didn't know how I was going to survive. In those moments, the only thing that really seemed to help was putting my total faith in Jesus. It was difficult for me to put my faith into words at the time; I still didn't know what it was, and I hadn't read the Bible or become familiar with organized religion. But I knew that when I needed help, Jesus was listening to my prayers. Praying to Him was an enormous comfort when nothing else seemed to help.

Four months passed. I remained numb and dead inside. It still felt like I was walking around with my arms and legs missing, with my skin ripped off, bleeding and raw.

It was very lonely. How would someone know I was suffering like that? How would anyone realize I was like the walking dead? This ignorance is something we're all guilty of. We look at people and judge them without having any idea of the pain they're experiencing. When I was a girl, my mother taught me to be kind to everyone, and I've always tried to be sensitive to other people. But Carlos' affair changed me. Since it happened, I've made a point of being kind to everyone – the clerk at a hotel, the range master at a competition, the waiter serving my dinner, a person on the street who smiles at me. Kindness is a great gift and one I believe comes directly from God.

Since I struggled to talk to other people about my pain, I kept asking myself: How is the love ever going to come back? Does it come back, or is it dead forever?

Carlos didn't provide any help. He has such a "go with it" personality that whatever I suggested, he said, "OK." When I said we should get a divorce, he said, "OK." When I asked about our assets, he said, "You keep them all." When I said we needed a lawyer, he said, "You pick one." It was frustrating. I needed him to be active. I needed to know what he wanted the next steps to be. Maybe, I thought, divorce truly was the best option. I just couldn't see how I would ever again love Carlos in the same way.

Around this time, I got lunch with a friend of a friend. This woman was recently divorced herself. During our time together, I saw how stuck this woman still was on certain things that had happened. She was living in the past. Seeing her, I thought: I don't want to be stuck on this for the rest of my life. Life goes so quickly, and if you waste too much time, your life will escape you. That's what was happening to this woman, and it could happen to me. I knew I needed to move on. I just didn't know how.

My therapist and I discussed the possibility of remarriage. If Carlos and I got divorced, I assumed I would eventually get remarried. But I think about marriage in terms of an investment. Love grows over time; your shared experiences are like interest, which pay dividends down the road. If I were to remarry, I'd be restarting that whole investment. Carlos and I had been married 28 years. I'd earned my place in the marriage, and I'd fought hard for our investment. I'd put in too much to give up now.

But if I were to move forward with Carlos, I knew I couldn't do so with anger in my heart. I had to forgive him. When someone hurts you, forgiveness is maybe the hardest thing to do. But it's also the only way forward; otherwise, you never get past what hurt you.

To forgive Carlos, I knew I had to make my heart bigger. I needed to get past my anger.

心平

For anyone who's been hurt in such a way, the road to forgiveness is very long. There are steps forward and steps back. Sometimes, steps back can lead to unexpected steps forward.

Around the end of the summer, I hit a point where I didn't really feel in control of my actions. I was so hurt and disoriented. The world still seemed dead around me. It was taking Carlos some time to end things with the girl. I understood that this was because he's a kind man and didn't want things to be too hard for her. But my patience was reaching its end.

I approached my former instructor at De Anza College, the police officer, and asked him if he could find this girl for me. It's not a moment I'm proud of, but it's a moment that I think a lot of people who've suffered similar pain have experienced. You feel desperate; it's like you have no choices left. In retrospect, I'm not ashamed of how I felt. Just as you have to forgive the other person, sometimes you have to forgive yourself, too.

The instructor told me he didn't do that kind of thing. But a week later, he called back and asked if I'd like to come down and help him with a class for rookie police officers. He wanted to demonstrate how lethal ordinary citizens can be with a gun.

I'd never thought I could have a lot to teach about shooting. Despite my training with Jim O'Young, and the competitions I'd attended, I wasn't yet a great shooter. And I hadn't shot much since May; after learning of the affair, I was too focused on surviving to shoot. What could I possibly teach a bunch of police officers?

In the end, I accepted his offer but knew I needed to prepare. I wanted to do the best job possible for the officers, to help them be better equipped for their jobs. I spent every day practicing and spent much of my free time thinking about how to do the best job possible for the new officers.

A lot of people would've approached this as a one-time, forgettable thing. They would have shown up, gone through the motions, and that would've been that. But if someone asks me to do something, no matter how small the task, if I agree to do it, I'm going to do it 100 percent. I don't believe in committing yourself if you're not going to be fully devoted to something. So even though it was just a class for new police officers, I treated it as seriously as I would have treated a new professional opportunity.

I went to the class and did well. When I came home, a strange thing happened – the pain returned, like a wave hitting me. But with it came a revelation: this renewed pain meant that, for a while at least, the pain hadn't been there. While training for the class, I'd been so focused on shooting that there wasn't room for the pain to get into my life.

心平

In September, shortly after the training class at De Anza, I went on a walking tour in France's Bordeaux Valley, a region of rolling hills, lush fields and vineyards, and deep river valleys. I couldn't stand being at home. Carlos knew I needed time to heal, and we thought it might be good for me to get away. Of course, I analyze things to death, so maybe this wasn't the best idea! But I needed to be somewhere other than home, and this was a chance to do that.

My mother took me to the airport to see me off. She told me she couldn't believe how thin I was. Mom often cooked for me to keep me healthy, so coming from her, this was a sign of her concern.

That trip was the first time I'd ever traveled abroad by myself, and I was completely disoriented. In France, at the train station, I went to the wrong section. I ended up falling asleep with my legs over my bags. When I left the hotel to find food, I got lost on the way home.

Despite these struggles, France was beautiful. We walked from small town to small town, covering 12 miles a day. As we passed through fields filled with dry, dead sunflowers, I imagined how they looked when the sunflowers were in full bloom, like a Vincent van

Gogh painting. I met artists. I told some women – all of them single – about what had happened with Carlos. I walked through Paris, too, and had one of the best desserts of my life.

Yet, I couldn't fully appreciate the beauty. I was still so wounded and empty inside. It was like that moment when I was driving to the range and saw the world outside looking cold and dead. My inner sadness affected how I felt about the world around me. Even prayer wasn't dispersing the cloud of sadness over my life. Asking God for help enabled me to survive, but I didn't want to live the rest of my years just surviving. I wanted more.

Around this time, I remembered something my therapist had told me during one of our first sessions. I'd asked her, "When will I start to get over this?"

She'd responded, "When you become good at something."

This reminded me of something Carlos had told me when I was only 18. I'd grown up with a huge inferiority complex. Again, this was partly due to my mother, who constantly told me I would need great inner beauty, because I didn't have much outer beauty. She wasn't trying to be mean; she was trying to help me adapt. She thought she was offering good advice. Carlos was the first person I'd told about my inferiority complex, and he also told me I'd get over it when I "became good at something."

And yet, there I was, 30 years later, and I was still trying to discover what that thing was.

Returning from France, I found life at home unchanged. I still wasn't able to move forward; the pain and anger remained. But a whole summer had passed. The pressure was on me now. I needed to do something to help myself move forward, or I was going to get stuck. That push wasn't going to come from outside.

Of course, Carlos was trying. He'd been working to, in his words, "earn back his brownie points" by doing nice things – getting me gifts and flowers, taking me out for dinners, picking up Austin from school. He and my therapist had decided that the thing I enjoyed most was deep powder skiing, so he took me to a resort in Utah that was supposed to have some of the best powder in the country. It didn't, but Carlos wasn't deterred. He was still a bundle of energy, constantly organizing activities in the hopes that they would help us return to normal.

The summer before I went to France, he decided we should all go skydiving. It was something he'd always wanted to do, and he thought it would be a good family activity. Austin was too young to go, but Carlos, Shane, and Christina went in the first plane, and I was right behind them on the second plane. We had a day of instruction and then jumped on our own from 13,000 feet. When I fell out of the plane, I remember looking up and thinking, "Wow, so many legs!"

But at the end of the day, even jumping out of a plane couldn't shake me from my numbness.

I appreciated how hard Carlos was working, but I truly didn't know if the love was going to return. I didn't see how it could, honestly. But I also knew I couldn't go through life like I'd gone through France, unable to fully appreciate the world's beauty. It would be a waste of God's greatest gift to us.

Amid all my sorrow and analysis, I began to understand certain things, too. The first was that only I could be responsible for myself – for my well-being, but also for my pain. I couldn't let anyone else be responsible for me.

I also learned that life doesn't work on your schedule. It happens on God's schedule. No matter how hard you try, it's out of your control. And when God presents opportunities, you have to seize them. You might not feel ready, but if God opens a door, there might only be one chance to step through. I'm not sure if I knew this consciously at the time, but subconsciously, I knew I had to keep moving forward. Even if I couldn't see the path, I had to trust that if I moved, God would show me the way.

In some ways, I think Carlos understood better than I did that sport shooting would be the thing that helped me heal. After seeing me during the De Anza class, he encouraged me to go shooting – to practice with Jim O'Young and go to matches. I hadn't yet considered that shooting could be a path forward, but I began to wonder if maybe sport shooting was the thing I was supposed to be good at.

THE RIGHT DIRECTION

Jim was still calling me and asking if I wanted to shoot. He would call and suggest a match – maybe a Steel Challenge – for the weekend. I started joining him, either for the matches or practice trips.

Like most people, Jim had no idea what was going on inside me. I preferred it that way. My private life is just that – private. And in a sport like shooting, people are already suspicious of women. Even today, there aren't many women involved in the sport, and there were even fewer back then. Again, a lot of people assumed you were either there with a man, or you were trying to meet one. I didn't want, or need, people knowing about my personal life. It would be even more of a distraction.

What all this meant was that I'd be standing next to Jim, shooting, and I'd be completely dying inside, but he would have no idea.

One of the first big competitions I did after I discovered the affair was the International Practical Shooting Confederation (IPSC) match in Richmond, California. Carlos thought IPSC would be fun for me, because it involved a lot of moving, running, and jumping over and around barriers. Or maybe *he* just thought it looked fun. Unfortunately, the event in Richmond was really macho. I wasn't the most popular person there, because I'd ask the guys for advice – and then I'd beat them in competition! Some guys liked to say things like, "Oh, Vera's just here to meet men." I'd think to myself, "You think I'm looking for men like *you*?"

Despite the bad experience at Richmond, I ended up shooting a lot of IPSC events, such as the Golden Gate Championship and the National IPSC Championships at Berry, Illinois.

Unfortunately, the setup wasn't a good match for my skillset. IPSC events included so much running and jumping, you almost had to be a track star to succeed! Once, at Richmond, where I'd applied for membership, a match was cancelled due to weather. A championship shooter's brother came over to me and said, "You don't help enough." I was still relatively new to IPSC, and although some shooters helped to move the obstacles around on certain stages, I didn't know enough about the discipline to design a stage; I was worried I'd make a mistake. I also couldn't drive a tractor around, which was how the heavier equipment was moved.

To me, with my limited exposure to the sport shooting culture, the men in IPSC seemed particularly macho, and the event involved a lot of wear and tear. Although I was doing well place-wise, often scoring as top woman at the club matches, I didn't feel like I was shooting at my best. The running and jumping didn't help my accuracy, and my body was too slightly built to handle the beating it took from IPSC over the long term. Because I wasn't making a lot of progress and didn't see much of a future in it, I started to think IPSC wasn't my thing. I cancelled my membership at Richmond.

Jim O'Young knew I wasn't happy with IPSC. He was a great teacher, and from a shooting standpoint, he understood his student. He said his job was to "help fix my guns," but he was also my eyes and ears. He kept me connected to the larger sport shooting community and informed me of any rule changes. Because he knew IPSC didn't fit my skillset, on his advice, I signed up for the American Handgunner's World Man-on-Man Shoot Off in 1995 in Montrose, Colorado. Because this was a huge match – it would be for a world title – I asked Carlos if I could go to Colorado for a week to learn about and prepare for the competition. This was a big step for me: It would establish the need for me to travel on my own to prepare for competitions, which I hadn't done before – and I'd be doing it with Carlos's full support. He said it would be fine.

The trip was important. The Shoot Off was a different kind of shooting from IPSC. IPSC is like what SWAT teams do in training. Along with all the running, there's a lot of kicking down doors and shooting through windows. The Shoot Off is more like the high-noon draws you see in the movies: You and another competitor shoot side by side, aiming at two sets of steel targets downfield. Each competitor is shooting at one set of targets. It's a competition that tests both speed and accuracy. It's also a fun event for spectators, because there are 15 stages, each with a different setup. Some targets are shaped like stars, others like bowling pins. Each shooter has six targets downrange, and there are two targets in the middle. The first shooter to hit the six targets and his or her middle target wins the string.

The setup wasn't the only new challenge. Some of the best sport shooters in the world were going to be competing in Montrose, including the top-ranked female shooters. One of the best was Kay Clark-Miculek, a great shooter in her late 30s. She also had a new child. Kay and I had competed against each other before and had become casual acquaintances. I once watched her toddler at a dinner Jim O'Young hosted so she could have time to eat. Another top shooter at Montrose was Julie Nowlin, a three-time Shoot Off Women's champion. She was in her early 20s.

I was 49. I knew that if I was going to be competitive against the younger, more accomplished shooters, I had to diligently prepare. Not only was I unfamiliar with the setup, but at that point in time, I was a nobody in the sport shooting world. The best shooters were Grand Masters. Just behind them were Master Class and Class-A shooters. And then there was me, a Class-B shooter.

When I arrived in Montrose to train, it was a beautiful sunny day. The very first string I shot, I missed three out of the six targets – with the ranch's owner/match director watching! From that first training session, I knew the competition was going to be difficult. It was all about speed and accuracy, and I'm not a good speed shooter. I've always been very accurate, but I need to take my time and be precise. Still, I was going to train relentlessly to improve.

And, very slowly, I began to get better.

After one week of practice, I started to get the hang of the Shoot Off. I was feeling more prepared for the competition. I'd had a good week of practice. The range's owner, who'd seen my struggles on my first day at the range, even remarked on how much better I'd gotten by the end of the week.

The weather helped my preparations. It had been warm, sunny, and in the 70s. But just when I was preparing to leave for home, the weather changed. I opened my hotel room door and saw snow on the ground. I closed the door, went back inside, sat down on the floor, and cried. I realized I didn't want to leave. I'd been so immersed in practice that I hadn't felt pain. I sighed, pulled myself up, and got in my car to head back to the airport.

But then I drove in the wrong direction. Subconsciously, I didn't want to go home.

心平

A few weeks later, I was back in Colorado for the Shoot Off. Thanks to my diligent preparations, I shot well in the competition but not well enough to finish among the top women. Still, I was satisfied that I'd shot the best I could under the circumstances. I'd proved to myself that I could learn an unfamiliar format and improve dramatically in only a few weeks' time. I'd also learned I needed to work harder if I wanted to reach my full potential.

Perhaps most importantly, the days when I was on the range shooting were days I felt myself healing. For a few hours at least, I was too busy and focused to feel pain. I began to think that God had laid out a path for me. I just had to find the courage to continue following it.

Counterclockwise from top: The author, Vera Fang, and future husband Carlos Koo, set sail in the Baylands Nature Preserve, Palo Alto, CA in 1966; Vera takes a real estate call while living in Singapore in 1980; Vera poses on a balcony at Escondido Village, Stanford, CA in 1967.

Clockwise from left: Vera (right) poses with parents Stella and Kai, sister Su, and brother Kim in 1953; Vera (middle) and Carlos with family friend, Professor Edith Young, at their 1969 wedding; Vera (right) with Stella, Kim, and Kai at Fisherman's Wharf, San Francisco in 1979; Vera (right) holds son Bryant while Stella embraces Vera's daughters Christina and Shane at Christmastime, 1976; Vera (third from left) holds Shane at a dinner party at the home of Professor Young (front) with Carlos (left), Kai (back left), Christina (middle), Su and Su's daughter Nicole (center), Su's husband Lowry (back right), and Stella (right) in 1975.

Left: Vera competes in the Practical Event during the 2018 World Action Pistol Championship, Hallsville, MO; Above: Vera holds her custom competitive-shooting gun during the 2012 Action Pistol Bianchi Cup Championships, Columbia, MO.

Counterclockwise from top: Vera annouces her retirement after shooting her last Bianchi Cup in May 2018, Columbia, MO;
Vera appraoches the Barricade Event during the 2018 World Action Pistol Championship, Hallsville, MO;
Vera holsters her pistol during the Moving Target Event at the 2014 Bianchi Cup Championship, Columbia, MO.

Counterclockwise from top: Carlos and Vera (center) get silly with granddaughters Aly, Ashley, Mia, and Annika in 2010; Vera with son Bryant at Memorial Park Cemetery, CA, where he was laid to rest six weeks later in 1977; Carlos and Vera (middle) at a friend's home with children Shane, Austin, and Christina in 1986.

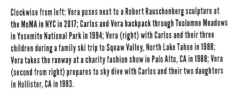

Clockwise from left: Vera poses next to a Robert Rauschenberg sculpture at the MoMA in NYC in 2017; Carlos and Vera backpack through Tuolumne Meadows in Yosemite National Park in 1994; Vera (right) with Carlos and their three children during a family ski trip to Squaw Valley, North Lake Tahoe in 1988; Vera takes the runway at a charity fashion show in Palo Alto, CA in 1988; Vera (second from right) prepares to sky dive with Carlos and their two daughters in Hollister, CA in 1993.

GETTING STRONGER: NOVEMBER 2013

By the time the 2013 NRA's Women's Leadership Forum arrived, I was walking under my own power. The only hitch was that I had to buy new shoes: My right foot was still so swollen, I needed a size bigger. It was a wonderful conference, and I met a lot of women who were interested in sport shooting. I felt good about how many more women had joined the sport since I began competing in the 1990s. It's still a male-dominated sport, but women are starting to make their mark.

I'd hit my recovery target for the conference, but I knew my next challenge was going to be even more important. I needed to go prone – to go from a standing position to lying down – in competition. This would be one of the most difficult parts of my recovery. Walking is easy. If you have to limp a little, you can still walk. But to shoot well while going prone, you have to get down on the ground without thinking; you need total confidence in your body and its movements. If there's even a shred of doubt in your mind, you're going to lose valuable time, and you might not finish your shots. If I was going to compete at the 2014 Bianchi Cup, I needed to have total faith in my body's ability to go prone.

I began preparing to go prone even before the conference. While I was still in my boot, I would take it off and walk around the living room on my knees. I had a large, worm-like scar on my knee from the surgery. I wanted to get used to putting pressure on that scar so it wouldn't bother me when going prone in competition.

Strength and confidence were a big part of my recovery, and I started to work with a trainer to build back the strength I'd lost over the months of inactivity. I also continued to eat, eat, eat. During the difficult time of my recovery, I relied on my familiar beliefs about diet and eating a lot to build back my body and its strength. I ate fruits and veggies and big, healthy steaks. As part of my usual training regimen, in the three months before the Bianchi Cup, I ate 44 14-ounce steaks to build up the muscle strength I needed for the competition. I started loading up on protein even earlier, too, to help with my recovery.

As I trained for my first competition in more than nine months – a club match in Southern California – I didn't know if I was going to be able to confidently go prone or not. My future in the sport hung in the balance.

GETTING STRONGER: PART II

After my first appearance at the American Handgunner's World Man-on-Man Shoot Off, my marriage with Carlos still hung in the balance, too. But for the first time since I'd found out about the affair, I was beginning to see a way forward.

Since I'd started sport shooting, our relationship had shifted. Carlos had always been a loving husband, one who wanted me to be happy, but he'd never found himself in a traditional support role. With the growth of my sport shooting career, Carlos found himself suddenly being the supportive partner.

He was good at it. He not only supported me going on training trips, but he would organize every aspect of them. He'd book my flights, rental cars, and hotels. He'd make sure I was taken care of.

Over the years, in addition to his many hobbies, Carlos had gotten his pilot's license and learned how to fly a single-engine plane. Sometimes, while I was away at a competition or on a training trip, Carlos would fly in his plane to pay me a visit. I think he was sort of checking up on me – there were a lot of men at these events, after all – but he also was coming to help make me comfortable. He knew I missed the great Chinese food from the Bay Area, so he'd bring some with him. The food helped me keep up my strength, and it helped Carlos keep winning back his brownie points.

My second year at the American Handgunner's World Man-on-Man Shoot Off Championship was 1996. Entering the competition, my game plan was still solely focused on shooting my best in comparison to my own skills. I didn't plan on beating anyone – I never do. I knew that the timing of my first shot was going to be critical to shooting well. I needed to be fast; but more than speed, I needed to be precise. If I focused on the task at hand and shot my best, then the competition would be a success whether I won or lost.

To the surprise of a lot of people there, I advanced through the first 15-stage match and reached the finals, where I would be shooting against the best female shooters in the world. I knew I couldn't start thinking about winning or losing. I just had to stay in my zone. In fact, I was so intensely focused that I don't remember much about the match, except that I wore a pink hat, black shirt, and white shorts. The only other thing I remember is that right before the match started, my opponent looked over at me.

The fact that I don't remember anything meant I was as focused as I could be. I was so focused, I ended up winning.

You'd think this would have been a huge moment for me. It was my first world championship title, after all. My friends were hugely excited. That evening, during a celebratory dinner at an Italian restaurant, Jim O'Young stood up and announced to the whole restaurant that I was the World Women's Shoot Off champion. Jim's a high-energy guy, and he can do unexpected things like that. He didn't have any idea what I was going through in my personal life; I don't think he knew that I was still hurting inside. Instead of feeling elation over the victory, I felt numb.

Despite his outburst, Jim noticed something wasn't quite right.

"Vera," he said, "you don't even seem happy about winning."
I said, "I couldn't feel anything."

心平

In hindsight, I didn't have any feelings because I effectively shut them off. I was so focused on the final of the Shoot Off that there was no room for any other emotion. If any of my feelings about Carlos or life at home had crept into my mind, I might have faltered. I needed clarity of thought to compete at my best. But after the competition, there was an emotional hangover. I remained in that shut-off state for two weeks following the competition.

I didn't realize it at the time, but this period of total focus is my best state for competing. It's when I can block out all other distractions, be they personal or professional, and focus only on shooting. In fact, I've figured out how much a thought – a single thought – can affect me in a competition. Two words is about .27 to .32 of a second. Four words is nearly half a second. And a whole sentence? Well, if I have a whole sentence worth of thought during a competition, I might miss the target.

This kind of total focus contradicts my natural personality. As an art major, I'm a right-brainer, a highly emotional person. But this is one of the things about shooting that is appealing – to succeed, I have to control my emotions entirely. It's an odd predicament for me, but I think God put me in this situation to learn how to control my feelings. I can't do it all the time, but the attempt to do so has made me a more disciplined, self-controlled person. I have God to thank for that. Through an enormous trial, He taught me something.

After the competition in Montrose, although I was now an American Handgunner's World Shoot Off women's division champion, my life in California hadn't much changed. I went back to my more natural role as a supportive wife and mother. I didn't talk much about my shooting, and my family didn't quite understand what a big deal my win had been. Even though Jim O'Young told Carlos, "That win was a big enchilada," I don't think Carlos really believed him.

Carlos finally understood a few months later, when the latest issue of *American Handgunner* magazine arrived. I knew I was going to be in the issue, because they'd asked me to send them two photos – one of myself and one of my family. When both appeared in the magazine, Carlos was surprised – and then he sort of understood how big my win had been.

As a rule, though, I don't like talking about my achievements in sport shooting. Even as I was getting better and winning bigger competitions, I tried to stay humble and quiet. I think there were a few reasons for this. One of them was that there were a lot of egos in "the boy's club". A lot of the men could be very sensitive about getting out-shot by a woman. I didn't want to step on any toes, so I kept relatively quiet.

At home, I tended to stay quiet for the same reason. It's not that Carlos has a big ego, but we've always had roles. He's been the more outgoing, forward person, while I tend to be more supportive. I was worried that if I suddenly became the person who was getting a lot of attention, it might make Carlos uncomfortable.

In a lot of ways, my entire life had trained me to not stand out. This all leads back to my mother, who always stressed that my primary role was to support my family. It was what traditional Chinese women did. She'd done it through her mysterious younger years, which were still clouded in mystery, and she did it after moving to a foreign country, where she knew almost no one. She expected me to fulfill the same expectations.

But one of God's gifts to me was a life in America. In America, it's possible to be whatever you want. People here aren't bound by old traditions or superstitions. My life wouldn't have been possible in any other country on Earth. I never would've stepped out of my supporting role.

Of course, Carlos never wanted or demanded that I simply support him. He's always viewed our marriage as a team effort, and that's why he supported my shooting – even if he didn't know what a big deal it was. Not only did he buy my guns and organize my travel, he was – and is – always there for me to call when the pressure builds over a long competition and I feel like I'm going to break.

In a big way, my life with Carlos actually prepared me for the pressure of sport shooting. In an event like the Shoot Off at Montrose, you're facing an incredible amount of pressure. You're alone out there, with just your gun and the targets, and you're facing one other opponent. My life with Carlos, right up until I began sport shooting, was very high pressure. We were constantly putting out fires. As soon as we put one out, another started. The pressure of living with Carlos, whether at work or at play, had built my personality to the point where it could handle a lot of stress. Being out there shooting wasn't any more difficult than spending 20 years fighting to get a business off the ground, or trying to learn to water ski in the morning and then going on a seven-mile backpacking trip in the afternoon. (And we'd have to come back down the next morning!)

Just as my life before shooting prepared me for the sport, shooting was helping me heal after the affair. Following my win, and after seeing my photos in the magazine, I actually felt pretty good. Sport shooting had built up my self-esteem and self-reliance. I'd achieved something that people said wasn't possible.

I've always made long-term goals, because I like projects that take a lot of time. My competitive sport shooting wasn't a short-term project. I'd won one event. But it's possible to get lucky and win once. I wanted to keep improving, to shoot better the next time than I had the time before. If that meant winning another title, great, but I wasn't shooting for titles. I was shooting to improve.

And I was starting to think that maybe sport shooting really was the thing that I was supposed to be good at.

SOMETHING BIGGER TO FOCUS ON

After winning the Montrose Shoot Off, I needed something bigger to focus on. That's where the Bianchi Cup came in.

Founded in 1979 by a former law enforcement officer, the Bianchi Cup is an NRA-sponsored action pistol championship. It's regarded as one of the three major action pistol championships in the United States and has the largest purse out of any action pistol event in America. It's probably the most prestigious title a pistol shooter can win.

I first heard about the Bianchi Cup in 1996. After my win at the American Handgunner's World Man-on-Man Shoot Off, I was still competing at a few, select IPSC events, because I hadn't yet found a good replacement for them. An imperfect competition was better than no competition at all, because it still gave me time to practice. But I knew I wasn't going to be shooting IPSC for much longer. I just needed to find my perfect discipline.

At the 1996 IPSC National Championship, I was squadded in a group that included eight top women sport shooters competing for the title. At the time, as with the American Handgunner competition, I was a B-class shooter. These women were all A-levels, masters, and grand masters. I was the lowest level shooter in the "super squad" at the championship. I even asked one of them how to shoot a particular run, and she gave me a look that seemed to say, "Are you serious? At this level, you're asking how to shoot a stage?"

But I didn't know any better. I had no formal coach, and I hadn't been shooting IPSC for a long time. In the end, she showed me how to shoot it.

Along with my other frustrations with IPSC, I didn't think it made practical sense to keep at it. If I was going to become an A-level IPSC shooter, I was going to have to practice really hard for at least a year. Due to the high power factor of the gun required in the discipline – it has a strong recoil – I was worried that becoming an A-level might lead to me getting injured. Looking at this potential scenario, and taking into account how I didn't really fit into the IPSC culture – an issue that had plagued me for a long time – I made a business decision. I would get better results if I switched to a shooting discipline that utilized my strengths: accuracy and consistency.

At the same 1996 IPSC National Championship, I had a conversation with Joe Dionisio, who was the father of one of the top male shooters, Jethro Dionisio. He said to me, "Vera, your draw is slow and you have no speed. You'd be better suited for the Bianchi Cup, because accuracy is supreme at the Bianchi." Joe Dionisio would help order my first Bianchi Cup gun.

I wasn't going to jump into a new form of competition without doing my due diligence. While researching the Bianchi Cup, I got in touch with John Pride, a former champion living in Southern California. If I was going to shoot the Bianchi Cup, he recommended I reach out to Mickey Fowler, a sport shooter who owns a big ranch in Mariposa with all the setups and stages for the Bianchi Cup. Mickey supposedly knew more about shooting the event than anyone. His ranch, I was told, would be a great place to familiarize myself with the format of the competition.

I called Mickey Fowler and asked him if he was taking students. At first, he said no, but when I told him my credentials, he said I should come out to his ranch to train with Ichiro Nagata, a well-known Japanese photographer and sport shooter, and a few of Ichi's "boys," young shooters from Japan who trained with him and lived in a cabin on Mickey's ranch.

In February 1997, I made the long drive out to Mickey's ranch, which was about four and a half to six hours from my house near San Francisco, depending on traffic and road construction. I was turning 50 that year. The drive wound through beautiful countryside, huge open fields that were mostly cattle ranches. Mickey's ranch was equally beautiful – a vast expanse of land with occasional forests of oak trees.

I was grateful to Mickey and his wife, Linda, for letting me come and practice on their range. They'd never met me, but they offered me their warm hospitality. This would help me learn the particulars of how to shoot the Bianchi Cup in an invaluable way. In my experience, most people in the shooting world are like this. They're generous to a fault. When I entered the sport, someone told me, "Though we're all competitive, we're also a community, and it's important that we help each other out." I've found this to be true. If my gun breaks, someone always helps to fix it. We look out for one another. We provide support in tough times and after difficult matches. I think it's something about the difficulty of shooting in the big events. You have to train so hard and for such a long time that only a certain kind of person can survive in this world.

During my first trip to Mickey's ranch, I stayed at a motel in Merced, an hour away. When I arrived at the ranch, Ichi wanted to test me, to see what my skill level was. I had to shoot six-inch white steel plates from 25 yards away. Thankfully, I'm both good under pressure and very accurate. I passed the test, and Ichi agreed to work with me. Every morning for a week, I would get up at 5:30 a.m. and get my equipment and food ready for an entire day of practice. I'd leave the motel at 7 a.m., and usually wouldn't return until 8 p.m. I shot 1,000 rounds a day for seven days straight.

Ichi and his boys taught me everything there was to know about shooting the Bianchi Cup. In the Bianchi Cup, there are four stages: the practical, barricade, moving target, and falling plates. They're all different challenges, but each one requires a lot of accuracy. For me, learning how to shoot each stage took a lot of trial and error. I tried all the different techniques that Ichi and his boys showed me. I kept what worked for me and discarded what didn't. Usually, they'd show me a technique in the morning, and I'd spend the rest of the day practicing that technique.

I worked incredibly hard. One afternoon, I remember that Ichi and the boys were jogging. They passed by the practical stage, where I was shooting, and said to me, "Vera, go home." They'd seen me there, on the range, shooting tirelessly for 11 hours. They thought I needed rest.

Most evenings, when I locked the gate, leaving to go back to the motel, a blanket of stars filled the sky. I had a Suburban stocked with a sleeping bag (in case the car broke down and I got stuck), six guns, 6,000 to 7,000 bullets, and a lot of food. I had an hour-long drive to the motel, and the road passed through very desolate terrain. Often, I'd be the only car on the road for the first 40 minutes of the drive. Sometimes, I could hear coyotes howling in the distance.

On those drives back to the motel or to the ranch in the morning, I often found myself watching the clouds, the various colors of the sunset, or gazing at the moonlit landscape. Many nights, a storm would be approaching. This accentuated the color of the clouds. Some of the most extraordinary clouds were visible during lightning storms, and I still remember looking in the rearview mirror and seeing the clouds lit from within by lightning.

Some of the sights made me remember being an art student and seeing Michelangelo's Sistine Chapel – all those peach clouds against baby blue skies. I thought he'd made it up! But seeing those clouds, I realized he didn't; they were real.

A lot of people don't realize how solitary sport shooting is. They think you go to the range with other people and maybe socialize a bit. But you spend so much time alone – on the range, commuting to the range. You have a lot of time to think. On those drives, I'd listen to tapes about the hundred most famous people – writers, composers, philosophers. Listening to the ideas of people like Socrates, Aristotle, and Plato, I realized that humanity hasn't changed that much over the centuries. We still think about the same things. We're still grappling with the same questions.

It reminded me of going into the Lacroix II caves in France to see the famous Paleolithic cave paintings, which were featured in Warner Herzog's movie *Cave of Forgotten Dreams*. When I saw the paintings, I burst into tears. I wasn't intending to cry. But the paintings were reminiscent of Picasso's modern abstract drawings. They were so similar. The form was captured in just a few lines. Seeing them, I thought: Although our material comforts are different across the span of human history, we think and feel in almost the same ways.

Although the solitude of those drives could be beautiful, it was also difficult. I was working hard, but I was away from my family and still coming to terms with Carlos's affair. I spent a lot of time during those drives crying, asking God, "Why am I doing this? What is the purpose of practicing for all these shooting competitions? What force is driving me?"

Despite how difficult it was, I kept pushing forward. I knew – and know – that God resides within all of us. It's when we face our darkest hours that we find Him. We find God when we're hurt, struggling, and alone, when it seems no one can help us. My dark hours had led me to Him. I knew He had a plan for me. As always, I just needed to follow it.

心平

In March 1997, I first flew to Columbia, Missouri, where the Bianchi Cup is held every year. I wanted to familiarize myself with the course ahead of the competition. In 1997, I would visit Missouri two or three times before the competition, which is held at the end of May. Most days, I was the very last person to leave the shooting range.

I practiced so intensely because I felt, since I wasn't on the professional circuit, I didn't have the same level of knowledge about the Bianchi Cup or how the competition was arranged as many of the other shooters did. I'd learned from my years doing Steel Challenges that to have consistency, you need to practice enough to develop the right muscle memories. In times of mental lapses, for a fraction of a second, your body will revert to that muscle memory and carry you through.

From Ichi, I'd also learned that timing is essential in the Bianchi Cup. In my many visits to the course, I was figuring out the precise amount of time I should have left at the end of each string. If I had .5 seconds left, it meant I had rushed a bit, sacrificing the quality of my shots. For me, the perfect amount of time to have left was .22 to .27 seconds. The margin for error was thin. A few stray thoughts here or there, and I might not get all my shots off in time. And the penalty if I failed was hefty.

To make sure no stray thoughts popped into my head during competition, I also worked on honing my concentration. I think of focus as a straight, horizontal line. Each thought that comes into my head is like a vertical line, cutting through my focus. At that point of intersection, where the two lines cross, there's a disconnect between the trigger finger and the brain. When I was younger, this disconnect was a fraction of a second, but as I get older, the disconnect grows longer. To shoot my best, my mind had to be clear of any thoughts.

This is one of the main difficulties with sport shooting. To shoot your best, you have to block out distractions on demand. Unfortunately, this isn't always possible. Thoughts creep in. If I could bottle total discipline, I'd be rich.

Most longtime sport shooters are inherently disciplined at controlling their minds. I know I can sometimes visualize in certain ways to make myself go to sleep. And I can blank out. Let's say I have an itch on my face or body: I can mentally move that itch to a place where I can scratch it. Once or twice, when I've been lying in bed, I've noticed I can mentally remove myself from my body. I believe that many people have this ability. Unfortunately, it's hard to control. If I don't constantly practice, I lose it.

In 1997, at my first Bianchi Cup, I was only beginning to understand how to focus intensely. I wasn't able to block out all the distractions. It was going to be a new competition on an unfamiliar course. But I'd prepared as best I could. And I felt ready.

THE BIANCHI CUP

The Bianchi Cup is held about ten miles outside of Columbia, Missouri, on a range nestled between lush, rolling hills. A small creek cuts through the center of the range. It's a very peaceful setting, but in the days before my first Bianchi Cup, the last thing I felt was peace. I was trying to be as focused as possible, while remembering everything I'd learned about the competition over the previous months. My head was like a computer stuffed with too much data.

Over the years, I've noticed a pattern in the way the Bianchi Cup unfolds for me. On the last day of practice, I'll be falling apart on the practice range. Most people who see me at this point tell me to calm down. But I remember what Mickey Fowler told me in my early years: Have a plan and execute it. Some people come to the Bianchi Cup to socialize, to attend barbecues and parties. This helps them relax. But I need to stay focused, and I know socializing will ruin my focus. This is just how I came to this life; it's how God made me. A lot of people think I'm a bit distant because of this, but I'm not. I'm just at Bianchi Cup to shoot the best I can.

Wednesday, the first day of competition, is like suiting up for battle. You must have everything prepared ahead of time. You need your guns and your ammo, as well as backup equipment in case anything goes wrong. You have to make sure you have clothes for all four seasons. You need water, food, and a cooler, as well as bug spray, a toolbox in case something in your gun breaks, and other supplies.

When I get to the range, I say to myself, "OK, for the next three days, you're going to go through hell. You're going to crawl, inch by inch, through this hole of suffering."

I'm not alone in feeling this way about the competition. In fact, I think most of the competitors who reach the same level I've reached feel like this. A grand master once told me that the week of the Bianchi Cup is the most miserable week of his year. Yet, he spends his vacation time to shoot at the event!

After one day of battle, you're wounded, but you get back to it. By the end of the second day, you're on the ground. You're really hurting, but you still have to pull yourself together to face the last day of the competition.

On Thursday night, I'm usually breaking down. I call Carlos. I'll find myself doubting my abilities, not sure I can get through the last day. If he's home, Carlos talks me through the suffering. If he's out of town on business, I'll sometimes call Jim O'Young to get his professional advice. As my teacher and mentor, Jim understands the psychological toll a competition like the Bianchi Cup can take on a person.

I usually spend a lot of Thursday night praying, asking God for the strength to continue. I know I can't do a competition this difficult on my own. If I'm going to survive it, I'll have to survive with God's help. I pray, asking for that help. Then I bandage myself up once more and go out there on Friday.

I've never found this pain or suffering to be unfair or too much. It's the price that has to be paid. If I'm not suffering, it means I'm not focused in the right way. It's the same almost every year. If you're going to compete at the Bianchi Cup, you have to accept that this is how it's going to be.

Of course, I didn't know any of this my first year. I thought I knew what the Bianchi Cup was going to be, but nothing could really prepare me for it. I was terrified, and praying was the only thing that seemed to help. When I was in my room, I'd immediately get down on my knees. I remember asking God for help. In May 1997, I asked, "God, I've never seen you before; could you give me a sign to show me you really exist?"

My first day at the 1997 Bianchi Cup, I was shooting the practical stage, which is when you shoot at two down-range targets from distances of 10, 15, 25, and 50 yards. I was scared but not nervous. There were many things I needed to do right during the competition, and I was extremely worried about missing one of them.

When the range officer brought my targets over, however, I saw that I'd shot a perfect score – 480. 40 of my 48 shots were in the X-ring, the four-inch center of the target that serves as a tiebreaker. It was a score I'd never before shot in any of my practice rounds, and it was a record-breaker for a woman at that time.

I cried the entire way back to the hotel. I'd never shot so well, so I knew it was more than I could do on my own. It was beyond my abilities. I considered it a sign. My prayer had been answered.

Despite that successful first event, my first year at the Bianchi Cup was almost entirely a learning experience. I'd prepared the best I could, but the real training is the competition itself. You learn something new every year, and it makes you want to come back and plan to do better the next time.

In 1997, I had no idea how I was doing. I don't pay attention to scores. I just keep to myself, stay focused, and shoot. An awards banquet is held on Friday after the competition. I never go to these banquets or dinners. Because I'm still very traditionally Chinese, I have no problem doing business with men, but I'm not very comfortable socializing on my own with them. But after competing in my first Bianchi Cup, one of Ichi's boys said, "You should go, Vera. You may get something. You can sit with us."

I got as dressed up as I could, and I went. Because I was invited, I sat with Ichi and his boys. When they announced the awards, I was surprised: I'd finished second in the women's competition and won first overall newcomer. The prize was $2,600 cash, by far the most I'd ever gotten in a competition.

When I found out about the awards, I knew I had to thank Ichi for all his help. I went up to his suite back at the hotel. Ichi is very traditional, and he values respect. So I bowed to him, and I said, "Thank you, Ichi, for teaching me to do Bianchi Cup." It was the best way I could think to show him how grateful I was.

Finishing second was a surprise. But it only made me want more. I'd shot my first Bianchi Cup and understood how it went. I couldn't wait for the next year to pass, so I could come back and hopefully do even better.

THE FIRST MATCH BACK

As 2013 became 2014, I was just trying to get back to the Bianchi Cup. I knew going through the competition was a little like going through hell, but I also knew there was no other place I wanted to be. The Bianchi Cup had become a way for me to measure my progress, to check in on my commitment and focus. Even as I've gotten older and can no longer reach the competitive heights I used to, attending the Bianchi Cup is still important. It means I'm continuing to set goals.

My first competition after my injury was a small club match in Southern California. Even though it was a low-pressure event, the first time I went prone, I tripped on my shooting mat, which is what you lie down on when you go prone. This stumble caused me to miss four shots. I knew I had to practice more if I wanted to go to the Bianchi Cup in good form.

Although some people, especially at my age, would've been discouraged by the long recovery process, I was very accepting. God had clearly planned for me to break my leg. I don't know why God wanted this to happen. But I don't question His plans for me. This goes back to Bryan's liver condition. I realized then that when I run into a setback, I accept what has happened and I move forward, trying to keep myself and my family well. Bryan would be in his mid-30s by now, so I've had this inclination for a long time.

My whole life has been: How do I survive this? How do I keep myself well? How do I move forward and meet my goals? Getting ready for the 2014 Bianchi Cup wasn't a foreign challenge for me. With God's help, I'd spent my entire life meeting challenges.

MY FAITH CONFIRMED

Preparing for the Bianchi Cup has consumed all my sport-shooting energy since the late 1990s. After my first time at the event, I was hooked. Joe Dionisio had been right: It was the perfect competition for me. It doesn't ask for great speed, but it demands a lot of discipline, accuracy, and practice. I can fulfill those requirements.

The only other competition I was still doing was the Steel Challenge, which meant I was going to spend all year preparing for two events. And I was constantly preparing. I'd take trips to Mickey Fowler's ranch and shoot 7,000 rounds in a week. I was shooting so much that my hands became swollen. I'd have to put them in ice during the middle of the night just to keep the swelling down.

At the same time, I had a responsibility to maintain my family and business life, too. Austin was still living at home. I wanted to be as present for his childhood as I'd been for our daughters'. Family time was always really important to Austin, so I made sure to keep fulfilling my duties. This meant having family dinners and preparing for the holidays. I made sure we had a beautiful Christmas tree, that the house was fully decorated, and that there were a lot of presents under the tree.

I know I wouldn't have had the strength to balance all of this on my own. I believe now that God set all of it up. I needed time to recover from the affair, and the Bianchi Cup provided me with that time. I was so focused on preparations that time passed without my really realizing it. As it slipped by, the pain of what had happened with Carlos continued to ease. Although I was still having trouble sleeping at night, without noticing it was happening, the two of us were rebuilding our life together. With each passing year, I could see how Carlos had prepared me for sport shooting. Because my family wasn't athletic, I wasn't used to any serious physical exertion. But thanks to all the sports Carlos and I had done – all the camping and hiking, the skiing and windsurfing and riding – I had grown used to hardship. I was no stranger to sweat and dirt. Carlos had toughened me up.

It was a good thing he did, because between sport shooting and our business, I was incredibly busy. It was exhausting. Our real estate business had improved, and I was working on the aesthetic parts of our commercial projects – carpets, paint, landscape design, etc. Although this was easier than the nitty-gritty work I'd done when we started, I still gave the work my all. I'd plant flowers at our house at midnight if I needed them for a party in two weeks. If I was leaving to shoot the next day, I'd pack until 2 or 2:30 in the morning and I'd wake up at 5 a.m. I was in my early 50s, but I still had the energy to cope with these workloads.

I know it was God who got me through this. At the time, my faith was still developing. I was still shaping my personal relationship with God. And although God had answered my first question, I felt there was another one I needed to ask:

"Is it true that if I ask, I will receive?"

He would soon answer that question, too.

心平

In the summer of 1998, I was with Jim O'Young at the Steel Challenge Championship in Piru, California. There were 11 of us on the squad, and we were preparing for a stage called "smoke and hope," during which you shoot five targets, from distances of seven, nine, and 14 yards. I believe that I wasn't born with a ton of natural speed, which has prevented me from reaching the highest levels in the speed shooting discipline. Jim, however, is a great speed shooter; he could do the challenge in 2.3 seconds. The best I could do was only 2.67 – and that was my fastest run, after a lot of practice. Even then, I was more comfortable doing it in an even three seconds.

Because Steel Challenge is a great spectator event – it's easy to see when targets have been hit – everyone was watching the shooters who were currently competing. I was eighth in our squad to shoot, so with everyone watching the competitors, I found a part of the range that was empty, a place where I could focus before my turn. I sat on a bench and prayed for energy to come into my body. I asked for focus. I asked for God's blessing to keep me calm.

I prayed for about 10 minutes. When I felt focused, I opened my eyes. I couldn't hear any other sounds. In fact, it seemed like I was entirely alone on the range. To my right, on the edge of the shooting bay, I saw Jesus, sitting on a big slab of stone. He was wearing an off-white robe, and his brown hair reached his shoulders. He said, "Vera, I'll walk you over."

I didn't react. The only thing to do was get up and walk with him – so I did. I have no idea how long we walked, but at first we were completely alone. While the two of us walked, it felt incredibly natural. I was totally calm and at peace. Then, after a certain amount of time, I saw legs. I didn't see any faces. Or, I should say that faces didn't register in my brain. This was a good sign – if I recognized faces or heard what people said, it meant I wasn't focused.

When I reached my bay, Jesus had vanished. I wasn't sure when He'd left, but I arrived right before I was supposed to shoot. I went through my checks and got ready. But as I was shooting, my gun jammed on one of the five runs I was required to make. (One run means you shoot, as fast as you can, at the five targets.) I'd never had a gun jam in a Steel Challenge before, and I knew it could be catastrophic – especially in a speed competition. But I cleared my gun faster than I ever had – or have. On the last run, I slowed down, and although I didn't miss any targets, I didn't think my time was very good. Yet, people clapped. When I checked my scores, I saw I'd had four perfect runs – four rounds without a miss. There was no way I could shoot four perfect runs, in a speed challenge, on a stage where I struggled to shoot perfect runs even in practice – especially after my gun had jammed. Once again, it was far more than I could've done by myself. I knew I had help out there.

On that day, I didn't tell anyone what had happened. I was worried people would think I'd hallucinated. In fact, I didn't tell anyone for a year and a half. But I knew, in my heart, that I had my answer. I also knew why I was working so hard: God was leading me.

Easter week of 1999 marked my most intense period of training for that year's Bianchi Cup. I now had two years of experience under my belt, and I felt I had a better understanding of the competition and what it was going to take to perform my best.

I was going to be spending the week training at Mariposa on Mickey Fowler's ranch. Austin, who was now in high school, was going on a school trip to Costa Rica. I told Carlos he should take his business trip at the same time, because no one was going to be home. We all dispersed, and I headed to the ranch. I spent seven days straight on the range, shooting for 10 or 11 hours a day, firing up to 1,000 rounds a day.

On my last day of practice, I was finishing up near the barricade stage. It was 6:45 in the evening, and I was trying to hurry, so I could leave the ranch before dark. I'd once gotten a flat tire on the deserted road back to my hotel. A Good Samaritan had come along to help fix it, but it made me realize that I didn't want to get caught out on that road after dark.

Because it was April, the days were getting longer, meaning I could stay out a bit later on the range. Right before I was set to leave, I stepped behind the barricade to pee. I looked up, and there, in the trees beyond the safety berm, I saw something. The trees were leafless, and the tree trunks were very dark. But there, on an oak tree, was a statue of Jesus. His face was turned about three-quarters toward me. His features were very Romanesque, his hair once more down to his shoulders. There was a crown of thorns on his head, and his arms were straight out to his sides, as if he was about to be crucified, although I didn't see a cross. I could see the muscles on his arms, all in perfect proportion. The cloth covering his lower body was textured.

My therapist had told me that it would be possible to see things like this when I was in deep meditation or prayer, but I wasn't in deep meditation. Yet, there He was. I'd been shooting in this very place for two years, and I'd never seen such a thing. The only thing I could think to do was kneel down and give thanks.

It was Easter Sunday.

I came back the next day to look again. And all I saw were the trees.

On future visits, I continued looking. Although I was able to see the shapes on the trees, I was not able to see Jesus again. Once more,

I didn't tell anyone what had happened to me – save Mickey Fowler, who I told years later, when I thought I might be leaving the sport. I figured I owed it to him, because I'd seen Jesus on his ranch. (And, of course, I changed my mind and continued to shoot!)

The 1999 Bianchi Cup was my third year at the competition. Although I never pay attention to scores, I believed that I hadn't yet shot my best at the championship. I was just learning how to peak at the right time, and I still wasn't sure I could achieve the kind of total focus I needed to shoot my best.

The first two days of the competition, beginning on Wednesday, went as I expected. I felt like a warrior, beaten and bludgeoned, still standing – but barely. By the time I got back to my hotel room on Thursday night, I didn't know how I was going to go back out there on Friday. I felt completely broken down.

I did the only thing I could think to do: I called Carlos in California. I was in a state of total breakdown. He gave me some encouragement, rallying me to go out and finish the competition.

With Carlos' help, and after praying to God for strength, I pulled myself together and went out on Friday ready to shoot my best. My detailed, disciplined approach to competition enables me to survive moments when I might otherwise break down. When I start to feel overwhelmed, I focus on the small details – how to pull the trigger gently and precisely, how to focus on the sights at the center of the target. I go through my motions, whether by dry firing or prayer. The repetitions of the sport help keep me sane; they're a good refuge when the tension ratchets up, as it does with each day of the Bianchi Cup. I went through my rituals and competed.

When it was over, I'd beat the other 12 female competitors to become the Bianchi Cup Women's Champion. I shot an 1894 out of a possible 1920. I won by a single point.

I'd like to say I was overjoyed; that winning the biggest event of my life felt like it changed who I was or altered the trajectory of my path in sport shooting. But the truth is, just finishing the Bianchi Cup is a reward in itself. Win or lose, you're so exhausted, so emotionally and physically wrung out, that all you can feel is relief.

When I got back to the hotel, I walked in the back door. I looked down the hall and saw someone who looked familiar. I said, "I think I know him."

Unbeknownst to me, after getting off the phone with me the night before, Carlos had been worried. All he knew was that I was all the way out in Missouri, falling apart. He'd felt helpless. He bought a ticket to Missouri so that he could, in his words, "Cart me home."

After a few steps down the hallway, I realized the man was familiar to me because it was Carlos. He said, "I came to help get you home."

All I could do was smile and say, "I won."

心平

Although I won in 1999, there wasn't the overwhelming sense of satisfaction many people would expect. The Bianchi Cup takes so much out of you that even though I'd won, I spent the first two weeks after the event in a haze – I'd say I was stunned stupid.

After I recovered, I returned to sport shooting. Later in the year, I was selected to be part of the U.S. Action Pistol Shooting team, which was going to compete in the World Action Pistol Championship in Hamilton, New Zealand. I also competed in the European Action

Pistol Championship in Tierney, Italy, and while I was there, I shot a 1912 – just shy of a perfect score, and the best I'd shot in a major competition.

If people had initially thought my win at the 1996 Shoot Off was luck, the sport shooters I respected most were beginning to take me seriously as a peer. But despite their growing acceptance, sport shooting remained overwhelmingly a man's world, and I still had to deal with the stray comment, like, "Vera's just here to meet men," or, "Your husband doesn't want you at home, so he sends you to shoot."

I'd always brushed these comments off with ease, and as I became more and more successful in the sport, these men looked more and more foolish. I didn't need to respond to them; my shooting talked for me.

Early in 2000, just as I began to focus my training on the upcoming Bianchi Cup, my family was once again shaken. On the evening of January 4, Carlos and I got an unexpected call. It was about my brother, who'd become a successful plastic surgeon living in Alamo, California. He'd recently bought a series of valuable antiques, including an antique bench chair, a Persian rug, and a Tiffany-style lamp, from a dealer he'd purchased from before. Delivery men dropped off the antiques and left, but they had apparently liked what they saw in my brother's spacious, well decorated house. They returned that evening to rob it. Unfortunately, my brother and sister-in-law were at home when the thieves returned, at 6:30 p.m. While resisting the robbers, my brother was shot and killed, and my sister-in-law was injured.

My brother and I talked from time to time – I would sometimes seek his advice on things – but we weren't especially close. In hindsight, this might well have had something to do with the family secret my mother kept from us, but which we all sort of sensed. Despite our somewhat formal relationship, though, the news shook me and my family. We'd been through tragedies before – my mother-in-law's illness, Bryan's death. But none of them had been so sudden and unexpected.

It was hardest for my mother. After my brother's death, she moved in with Carlos and me for two months. Although she was obviously shaken to her core, she also didn't seem quite right, aside from just the grief. She'd always been a very meticulous person, but during her time with us, she seemed distracted and forgetful. The teakettle would be whistling, and she'd be sitting on the couch, oblivious; she'd forgotten she put tea on.

I also was struck by the fact that when we all finished eating dinner, Carlos and Austin would immediately get up and leave the table. Normally, our family dinners would last two or three hours. We're a very chatty family. We all have so much to say that we usually spend dinners talking – and talking over each other – for hours.

Concerned by these developments, I took my mother to a neurologist. They told me she had early stage dementia and recommended we place her in senior or assisted living facility as soon as possible. Time would be of the essence, because it's extremely difficult to get a spot if you try to place an elderly relative too late, when the dementia has gotten worse and they need almost round-the-clock care.

I'm not the kind of person to put a job off, so even though we were still processing my brother's murder – and even though I was training for the Bianchi Cup – I immediately began looking for a place for my mother. Thankfully, she was still of sound enough mind that she was admitted into a regular home. She didn't fight the move, and because the dementia was still in its early stages, her behavior didn't suffer too much. She still wore makeup and nice clothes, as she always had. During her first year in the home, whenever I went to visit, she always had a lot of people coming to sit and eat with her.

The home was just seven minutes from our house, which meant I visited a lot. I'd hang my mother's medication on the fridge. She had old-age-onset diabetes, so it was important she take her insulin. The pills were always gone, so it seemed like she was taking them. All in all, it seemed like she'd adjusted to life in the home. Although our relationship had shifted – I was now checking on her, instead of the other way around – I felt good about how she was doing.

One night, about a year after she moved into the home, I went over just before I was supposed to leave town for a match. I popped in at 11 p.m. and found the lights still on. There was no sound, so I figured my mother had fallen asleep. Her medications were empty, so I started working on her pills for the next week. Before leaving, I popped my head into her bedroom to turn off the light. That's when I saw my mother, lying there, head on her pillow, eyes wide open. At first, I thought she was dead. But when I checked her pulse, she was still alive. I immediately called 911.

At the hospital, I found out she'd gone into insulin shock, which wouldn't have been possible if she'd been regularly taking her medicine. We found some of her pills in her purse. She'd put them in there to take throughout the day, but then she'd forgotten about them. When we talked to the manager of the retirement center, she said Mom sometimes wore two or three blouses at the same time and that she wasn't eating much. I wasn't thrilled with the management at the center – they should've paid closer attention and should have alerted me about this sooner – so we hired a personal caretaker to help Mom with her daily tasks and make sure she took her medication.

All of this was ongoing as I trained for the 2000 Bianchi Cup. Maybe it's not surprising I didn't win again, with all that was happening, but the fact that I'd competed and finished was still rewarding, even without a championship trophy.

MY FAMILY'S STRENGTH

With the 2014 Bianchi Cup drawing closer, I was running out of time to become comfortable going prone. I didn't know if I would be able to compete.

During my final months of training, I needed to dig deep into my reserves of strength. I've always been proud of my resilience and strength – not physical strength, necessarily, but mental strength. I can handle pain and suffering. I can work as hard as anyone. That stuff just doesn't bother me. Where, I sometimes wondered, did that persistence come from?

By this point, I realized that the father who raised me, Kai Fang, was not my birth father. There had been all those hints along the way – my father's parents teasing me, saying I wasn't a Fang; my mother affectionately calling me "little ugly duckling," because I didn't resemble my siblings; the fact that my mother had left her first husband and that she had no contact with her family.

It may seem strange, but growing up, I never questioned that Kai Fang was my father. He'd raised me as his own daughter, showing me love and compassion. I was never treated differently.

As my mother's dementia grew worse, however, she kept mentioning the name "Wu Grayling." It was a name I'd heard since my childhood, but I had no idea who he was. In her dementia, Mom often said, "You look just like him."

I wondered if she was referring to my biological father. If so, all the other facts started to make sense.

Around the same time, Carlos went on a business trip to Singapore. While there, he met with his aunt. She told him I must take after my father, who carried a gun and commanded soldiers. Carlos was confused. Kai Fang was a gentle man. Although he'd been a translator for the U.S. Marine Corps, he was not a shooter or soldier. He liked reading and listening to opera.

The next time Carlos saw his aunt, he questioned her. He asked if maybe Wu Grayling was my birth father.

His aunt had heard about my real father from Carlos' mother, who had spoken to my mother at our wedding. My mother believed in sharing family secrets, and had told Carlos' mother that Kai Fang wasn't my birth father.

Carlos' aunt told him there was no way Wu Grayling could be my real father's name. A portion of it, "Wu Gray," can be interpreted in Chinese as the word "turtle". Turtle has a few meanings in Chinese culture, but one of them is an insulting term for a man. It's like calling him a cuss word. My mother was referring to my biological father in a derogatory way, basically calling him a pimp.

Taking all of the facts together, Carlos and I have come to believe my birth father was a Chinese warlord who, as Carlos' aunt told him, carried a gun on horseback and commanded soldiers. Powerful men having concubines was part of Chinese culture in those days, and I believe my birth father had several concubines. Perhaps my mother was a concubine herself.

I also believe my mother had three children with this man, her first husband: the two children she left behind – and me. She was pregnant with me when she left him and ran off with Kai Fang, who had been tutoring the children born to my biological father's concubines.

Carlos believes my biological father must have been a persistent, dogged man, one who showed grit. He says this because I displayed these traits throughout my sport shooting career, and they're traits that cannot be traced to either of our families.

It's possible I inherited some useful qualities from my biological father. In the spring of 2014, with the Bianchi Cup fast approaching, I was drawing on my persistence and grit once more.

But I was also still benefitting from the love and generosity people had shown me throughout my career, and especially during my recovery. I was benefitting from all the people who'd taught me how to shoot over the years and all the people who'd made me guns or let me practice on their properties, like Mickey and Linda Fowler. I was benefitting from Jim O'Young's help, both as a mentor and during the early days of my recovery. I was benefitting, as I have for 50 years, from Carlos' unshakeable support and all the sacrifices he'd made to help my sport shooting career.

And I was benefitting from the love and kindness of my parents – the parents who raised me. My mother may not have shown grit and determination in her day-to-day life, at least as I knew her, but it took incredible courage to run away from an abusive husband, and to cut ties with her entire family in the process. My biological father must have tried to find her, and this is why she couldn't stay in contact with her family. She occasionally sent someone to make contact with them, but as far as I know, she never heard anything back. To do what she did, when she did it, was profoundly brave.

Kai Fang, the man who raised me, must have known I wasn't his biological daughter. But he loved me in the same way he loved his biological children. He spoiled me, taking me to beaches and on hikes. He showed me that family isn't just about blood; it's about love.

I'll probably never know the full story of my biological father, but even if I did, it won't change how I view my parents. Sing Tso was my mother, and Kai Fang was my father.

MY PEAK

The months leading up to the 2001 Bianchi Cup were calmer. My mother's condition had stabilized. She'd always been a survivor, especially considering her incredible past. No matter what life threw at her, she never complained. She just continued on as best she could.

We now had a caretaker looking after her, making sure she was taking her medicine. I was still visiting every week, and although it was difficult to see her so frail, I was grateful to still have her in my life – and especially grateful for everything she'd taught me.

As for Carlos and I, by focusing on our business and our routines, we'd managed to weather the storm of my brother's murder the way we'd weathered other storms: together. More than nine years after Carlos' affair, the two of us were finally back to "normal" – even if that normal was new and different from what it had been before the affair.

With life more settled, I focused on my practice. My goal was making sure that I peaked during the competition.

Two days before the Bianchi Cup, a warm-up match took place. Almost all the top competitors – male and female – took part. Although it was a warm-up, I told myself, "Take every stage seriously."

Even though it wasn't part of the main competition, I knew it was no time to let my focus or discipline lapse.

I achieved a state of total focus, where no outside thoughts crept into my mind. When I finished the last stage, I'd scored a 1920 – a perfect score, and the top score among all competitors, male and female. Afterward, many male shooters lined up to shake my hand – men who just a few years before thought I was a slight Chinese woman who was out of her league.

Two days later, while I was shooting in the main competition, a renowned gunsmith, Don Golembieski, who had built Bianchi Cup guns for me, approached and asked me a couple of times, "How are you doing?"

It was my habit not to speak with anyone at the shooting range during the championships, because I can't focus if I'm talking to people. When I didn't answer, Don asked me again, "How are you doing?"

Something in the interaction struck me. It was as if, all of a sudden, I remembered how totally out of place I was. With my upbringing, I would've never imagined being a part of the sport shooting world. And now, to actually *be* someone worth noting in that world? It was impossible to believe.

After that, I sort of stepped back. I said to myself, "Who are you to shoot a perfect score? You can't do that." Just as I was beginning to make a name for myself, I started to have doubts. It was the inferiority complex I'd had since childhood rearing its ugly head.

Despite this, I went on to shoot my best score in the Bianchi Cup – a 1910. I was once again the Bianchi Cup Women's Champion. But my doubts would persist.

THE "THREE-PEAT"

By 2003, I had further established my place in the sport shooting world. I was the two-time defending Bianchi Cup Women's Champion. *NRA Magazine,* wondering if I could "three-peat," put me on its cover – a huge and unexpected honor.

At home, things with Carlos weren't just back to normal. They were actually improving. He'd earned his brownie points and more. Although Carlos and I have been together for more than 40 years, I've never grown tired of him. He's energetic and funny; he makes my life better and more enjoyable by introducing me to new sports and feeding me the latest world news. Even after everything we've been through, I still love his company.

The fact that he and I were doing well again cast my future in sport shooting into uncertainty. I'd gotten serious about my practice and competitions after finding out about Carlos' affair. Throwing myself into the sport had been a form of therapy. Now that Carlos and I were doing better, maybe it was time to put my efforts into something else. I didn't need therapy anymore.

Although I'd won two Bianchi Cups in a row, I was worried I wasn't peaking at the right time. After I shot that 1910 and pulled back, it was almost like I had a psychological block. I couldn't shoot quite that well at Bianchi anymore. I had won again in 2002, but in 2003, I wasn't shooting my absolute best in the weeks leading up to the competition. I'd gotten close to perfection, and that voice, the one saying, "You don't belong," had risen up. Whenever I started to close in on a great score, the voice would strike, and I'd miss a shot.

I wondered, what was the purpose of continuing to shoot? Was I going to continue sport shooting indefinitely? Was I trying to get back to that place where I could shoot a 1910, or even a perfect score, at the Bianchi Cup?

I was also tired. It's difficult to stay in this sport – and even harder to stay on top. I work as hard at sport shooting as I do at home or at our business. People think that when I go to shoot, it's for fun, and when I go home, it's to rest. But I never really get rest. When I shoot, I'm totally there, giving 100 percent. And when I come home, I'm 100 percent devoted to my family, to being a wife. I still make sure the house is ready for big dinners and for the holidays. In 2003, I was supporting Carlos in our business, at functions where we had to entertain, and on business trips. And I was caring for my aging mother, whose dementia was growing worse.

I knew I was at least going to shoot that year's Bianchi Cup, but afterward, I wasn't sure.

I won the Bianchi Cup again in 2003, completing the "three-peat," but my doubts remained. For the first time since I'd begun sport shooting, my focus was wavering. And when I prayed about the matter, I didn't feel the same clarity I felt in the past. It was like I couldn't hear God anymore.

So I asked God my third and final question: "I don't feel as close to you as I once did. Did you leave me – or have I left you?"

心平

At the time, I was still visiting my mother at her home a couple of times a week, trying to help care for her in what ways I could. My mother had always been my closest friend and one of my closest confidantes. Even when I learned the secret she'd kept from me – about my birth father – it didn't change the love I had for her. My adoptive father had never treated me any differently than his biological children; he had loved me just as much. My mother was trying to protect us, so why should I hold that against her?

As her health deteriorated, I missed going out with her to talk and watch movies together. Watching her slowly decline was a potent reminder that no matter how healthy you are, time eventually gets to you. We can't stop aging, but with luck and grace, we can temper its effects if we stay busy.

As my mother was getting worse, a lot of my friends or their husbands were starting to retire – and some of them were bored out of their minds. They had nothing to focus on all day. In contrast, I was putting so much work into shooting that it was keeping me healthy, both physically and mentally.

My doubts about my future in sport shooting had persisted, and my mother's health and my friends slowing down all weighed on my mind. Around 2003, I began playing with the idea of becoming a motivational speaker. Asian-American culture tends to value being private; we keep our affairs to ourselves. People who perform public services tend to do so through professions that pay well – as dentists, lawyers, or doctors. I wanted more people from my culture to be openly engaged in the community. I thought getting my story out there and talking about my sporting successes could help inspire more people, especially women, to get engaged.

I found a publicist to help me. She would spread my story through writing a book and help me begin my career as a speaker. I took seminars on public speaking. My story might be useful to a lot of people, I thought. I wanted people to understand that you could come from one culture – in my case, a very traditional Chinese background – and through hard work and determination succeed in a totally different one. In fact, this very possibility seemed to capture the entire promise of America: Anybody can succeed at anything they want if they work hard enough. My life was the embodiment of the American dream. I am profoundly grateful to this country for providing me with the opportunities it has. And I have always wanted to share that gratitude with others. I thought public speaking might be the best way to do that.

Unfortunately, the more I attempted to be a motivational speaker, the more I realized how difficult it was. I couldn't even get my friends to work harder. How could I convince strangers to pursue their dreams? Plus, the publicist I'd hired to help tell my story was in over her head. Eventually, I sat down to talk to Carlos about all of this, to weigh my options. What else could I pursue?

"Think about how long it took you to reach this point with shooting," Carlos told me. "If you start something new, you'll be starting from scratch. Do you want to be doing that? Starting over?"

He was right. It had taken me more than 10 years of intense work and discipline to get to where I was in the shooting world. Another 10 years of hard work at something new, and I'd be nearly 70. Would I have the same energy then?

When I look back on this period, it's easy to see that I've been sport shooting long enough that, during certain periods, my motivations have changed. When I started, shooting was therapy. Now that I'm older, I do it because it keeps me healthy. It also keeps me from getting bored. The sport pushes me to my limits. And when things went stale for a few years in the mid-2000s, I kept going because, really, what else was I going to have time to get good at?

I also knew that the Bianchi Cup was and is a very strange event. It's a momentum game, so it's difficult to rest, take a few years off, and come back strong. If you take time off, your skills deteriorate. Sport shooting is a perishable skill. What makes the Bianchi Cup such a test is that it takes a certain amount of determination to stick with it. The people who win are usually people who have suffered through difficult years when things went wrong or they weren't motivated. It's a competition that rewards perseverance.

All of the experiences I'd had helped me make the decision to stick with sport shooting. If I hadn't considered taking up motivational speaking or had the bad experience with my publicist, I might not have stuck it out – just as the affair helped me to get serious about shooting. Once again, it became clear that I wouldn't have accomplished all of it on my own. Events happened exactly as they were supposed to, even if I couldn't see the path. I'd had help from God. Through these experiences, my questions had been answered. God has always been there, every minute of my life. It's only me who has moved away from Him.

With my final question answered, I began to think about getting baptized. As a child, I'd never had the opportunity; again, my family wasn't religious. But as I got older and grew more successful in the sport shooting world, I'd become more and more open about my faith. Initially, I hadn't talked about seeing Jesus. I was worried people might think I was hallucinating or even that I was crazy.

One of the events that encouraged me to be more open about my experiences was a trip I took in 1999 while at the World Championships in Italy. During my time overseas, I visited churches all around Florence, paying special attention to the frescoes, paintings, and statues of Jesus. When I saw Christ, I wasn't yet very familiar with the Bible. I didn't have a clear idea of how Jesus was supposed to look. But the Jesus I had seen was the same Jesus reflected in the Italian church paintings and statues. He was young, in his 30s, and Romanesque in his facial features, with shoulder-length hair.

As a former art student, I'm familiar with famous artists through the ages; they don't like to copy other artists' work. How, then, had all these artists portrayed Christ so similarly – and how had I seen the same Christ, despite a lack of familiarity with the Bible?

The more paintings I saw, the more I thought that these artists must have seen Jesus. It would explain their uncanny accuracy in portraying him. Seeing those paintings made me believe that far more people have seen Jesus than we think. They just don't acknowledge it for fear of looking crazy.

By 2001, I'd begun seeing an intuitive counselor who had studied theology in her younger days. She convinced me to spread my story. I told Carlos first and then began telling my friends. I told my best friend, Cecilia, who invited her two sisters over. She wanted me to tell them my story. One of the sisters said, "You were wise not to tell anyone this." She thought people might think I was crazy. But the other sister said she supported me. Cecilia later told me that this sister had seen Jesus, too.

These experiences deepened my faith. So, too, did all the times God stood with me during my matches or walked me through my lonely moments. During my first Bianchi Cup, I would pray constantly – I still do – and I remember the feeling of being surrounded by angels. I never saw them, but I knew they were there. I could feel them.

By realizing how much help I'd had and seeing how much God had pushed me, I eventually decided it was time to take the plunge and get baptized. I didn't belong to a church. In fact, I seldom go to church; most of my knowledge comes from religious TV stations like EWTN, a global Catholic television network, or from listening to Sister Angelica radio. I've always believed my faith is best expressed through my direct relationship with God and Jesus, as communicated through prayer. Through prayer, I get to know God. But when I talked to my sister-in-law about my desire to get baptized, she laughed and said, "Who is going to baptize you, since you don't belong to a church?"

I hadn't thought of this. I wasn't sure if God would make it difficult for me to get baptized. It was just a way for me to affirm to Jesus that I believe in Him. As I am somewhat ignorant of religious protocol, to me it was a very personal gesture.

Thankfully, I had an old friend, one of the women from my ladies' lunches, who was also looking to get baptized. She'd gone through a divorce and found God during her recovery. During one of my periods at home, I had a free morning before I went to shoot at the range near my house. Having almost gone through a divorce myself, I thought this friend could use some support. I went to the florist and bought a bouquet. Then I went to her house and gave her the flowers, and we talked. Near the end of the conversation, almost offhandedly, I mentioned I was considering getting baptized but didn't have a church. My friend said she was going to a church and that she was looking to get baptized, too. Her pastor agreed to baptize me if I went through two interviews.

In October 2003, I attended a service at the High Way Community Church in Palo Alto to be baptized by Pastor Dean Smith. I had attended the church before and liked its lighthearted atmosphere. It had lots of music and singing.

Four people were scheduled to be in the baptism ceremony that Sunday. We each were asked to come on stage and talk about our experience with faith and knowing Jesus. I told the audience about the two times I'd seen Jesus. Then we all went outside and circled a big tank full of water. I wore a long white summer dress, with a black and white swimsuit underneath it. After the ceremony, I was happy.

I'd finally affirmed my faith in our savior, Jesus Christ, and God.

FINAL PREPARATIONS: SPRING 2014

As I prepared for the 2014 Bianchi Cup, I tried to go about my preparations the same way I always had, accommodating any necessary adjustments to my techniques with approval from my doctor. I stuck to my recovery diet and exercised constantly, including workouts with a personal trainer, who made sure I was strong enough to compete.

I pushed myself in practice, trying to simulate the pressure of a match. I also made sure that my leg would work when I went prone. I needed to adjust – to go down to the ground in a way that my leg could tolerate. It was slow progress, but it was progress. I went prone in my first matches back, even if it took much longer than it used to.

I'm not sure I could've done any of this without Carlos. He managed my schedule and drove me to and from my early doctor's appointments before I could drive myself. He often took me to Baskin Robbins after my physical therapy appointments. We'd gone to Baskin Robbins almost 50 years earlier, when we'd started dating. I still got the same flavor – pistachio almond. Carlos was a rock during my recovery.

In the months before the 2014 Bianchi Cup, I knew I would have to visit the range near Columbia. If I wanted to prepare as I always had, visiting the tournament site was an important step. But I was reluctant to go. I didn't know how I'd feel returning to the place where I'd been injured.

Still, if I was going to compete, I'd have to face that range sooner or later. And it was better if I faced it sooner, in practice, than later, during championship week.

CHANGES

Like all sports, sport shooting has evolved over time as the equipment and technology have changed. I've never really cared about the technical aspects of the sport. I can take apart my gun – an open category race gun, which includes about 30 parts, both big and small – clean it, and put it back together, but I don't understand the mechanics behind it. If my gun breaks, I am going to have to find someone else to fix it.

In 2006, changes were made to the rules governing action pistol competitions around the world. Before these changes, my gun had a slightly more than one-pound trigger pull. This meant you only needed the slightest bit of pressure to fire a shot – or to fire multiple shots in a short amount of time. It took years of practicing to gauge that weight perfectly, to get it right. The motion, the weight – it was all muscle memory. And by that time, I'd won six Bianchi Cup championships in a row, something no woman had done before – or has done since. I might not have been peaking every year, but I was breaking records for a woman in sport shooting.

After 2006, we moved to a two-pound trigger requirement at the Bianchi Cup, which meant I'd have to go into the competition with a 2.25 to 2.5 pound trigger pressure. This doesn't sound like much, but it required twice as much force to pull the trigger. Because I was no longer able to acquire a two-stage trigger for the new two-pound requirement, it was no longer a quick, easy pull on the trigger to get off a shot.

The change entirely altered the way I shot. Just as it took years to perfectly judge the 1.125 pound trigger, it took a long time to get used to the new weight and the one-stage trigger. I've figured out that it takes me two to five years to adapt to such changes.

Around the same time, I also started taping my fingers. After years of practicing and shooting approximately 60,000 to 80,000 rounds a year for the Bianchi Cup and Steel Challenges, my hands were starting to show signs of wear and tear. I thought the tape would ease some of the strain on my fingers. Unfortunately, it also dulled some of my sensations. I couldn't feel the trigger as cleanly as I once could.

When the problems in my shooting started showing up, I thought it was due to aging. By the time I realized it was the tape, I'd already picked up some bad habits. By then, four years had passed; these bad habits only worsened after the trigger weight change. As I tried to adjust, I doubled down on the bad habits. Suddenly, I couldn't go on autopilot from 10 yards away; I was dropping easy shots. I was having real problems with the moving target stage, where you shoot from different distances at a target that moves horizontally, from both left-to-right and right-to-left.

In 2007, for the first time in seven years, I didn't win the Bianchi Cup. Later that year, I was competing at the European Open Action Pistol Championships in Philipsburg, Germany. I was still adapting to the new trigger weight and still fighting my bad habits. I knew it was going to be a challenge going to Germany, purely from a shooting standpoint. But I also knew it was going to be tough culturally. Women in sport shooting are still treated as second-class citizens in Germany, or so I was told by a close friend, who had recently returned home from the country; she has a Ph.D. in psychology.

On my first day, one of the German guys came over and greeted me. He offered to help me practice by running my timer. I always struggle on the first day of practice, as I adapt to the new environment. He'd heard I was a very good shooter and was very disappointed by my performance that day. Another man tried to show me how to "properly" go prone. I do it my own way to avoid injury. Finally, the defending European Open champion was in attendance, and he behaved very arrogantly during his practice rounds. The general impression the German men conveyed was that I didn't belong on their level.

It would've been easy to fold, but shooting under pressure is when I'm at my best. During the match, it started to pour rain. Most people don't shoot much in the rain. At the Bianchi Cup, the rule is: if you hold out your hand and more than 12 drops fall on it per second, you don't shoot. At the World Championships in 2007, the ground at the plate range was covered in two inches of rain, and we were still shooting. My towel was too soaked to dry anything off.

But I've always practiced in rain. Someone once told me that sometimes you have to compete under those conditions, and I believed them. If I was on the range and it started raining, while everyone else packed up and went home, I kept shooting. I learned to block out the rain, the way I block out thoughts or crowd noise. The 2007 European Open Action Pistol Championship in Philipsburg was the first time all that practice in the rain paid off. While many of the other shooters struggled with the conditions, I managed to shoot well. I shot a perfect score on the plate range. I came in ninth out of 78 shooters, male and female.

After the match, the former Euro champ came over and shook my hand. He said, "Vera, I want to build you a gun." Unfortunately, foreign-made guns are difficult to get into the U.S., so I just bought two holsters from him instead.

The guy who timed me during my first, disappointing practice? He came over and shook my hand. Another shooter stood and shook my hand for 15 minutes while he talked with me. Although I was very accustomed to people dismissing me at first and then being surprised by my abilities, it still felt good to prove people's misconceptions wrong.

STILL STANDING

When I first set foot on the range in Columbia, Missouri, it was like returning to the scene of a great trauma. It's difficult to describe the feeling. I tried to push it away and to shoot as normal. But no matter how hard I tried to focus, I couldn't push thoughts of what had happened out of my mind. I missed some plates I normally wouldn't have missed. But I kept trying to steady myself. I knew that it was better to get it out of my system now, that this was a part of the recovery process, too.

When I made it through my first day at the range, it felt like a weight off my shoulders. But I knew the competition was going to be even more pressure. I didn't know if my body – or my mind – was up to it. My leg and foot still had a tendency to swell a little, especially if it was a very hot day. If I was going to shoot my best – or even shoot at all – I needed the weather to cooperate. And then I had to trust in my mind – and especially my body – to hold up.

I'd done everything I could to prepare. I'd listened to my doctors' instructions. I'd eaten everything I could. I'd kept my mind strong, even when my body was weak. I'd put my total trust in God. And thanks to His wisdom and the help of those closest to me, I'd been able to get back on my feet sooner than anyone expected. I'd hit every milestone I'd set for myself: going to the women's conference, going prone, and competing in my first competition after the injury. Now I'd faced down the scene of my injury, and although it had shaken me, I was still standing.

I'd made it this far. All that remained was competing in the Bianchi Cup.

THE NEXT LIFE

By the late 2000s, I'd become well known in the sport shooting world. This was a little strange for me, as I've always been someone who stays behind my husband. As the child of a traditional Chinese family, it was my responsibility to tend to my family and friends before I tended to myself.

Staying humble always has been very important to me. This is a product of my upbringing and of my faith. I am so dependent upon God for everything I have – for showing me the way and giving me His blessing to pursue shooting for so many years. I try to bring people gifts to show them love and respect. When I'm out with friends and family, I still try to stay quiet and not be the center of attention. Unfortunately, some attention is unavoidable when I go to a shooting event, but I don't want that attention to spill into my life outside of shooting.

In 2008, I won my last Bianchi Cup title. It was my eighth title overall, including the six in a row I won from 2001 to 2006. But this title seemed, in some ways, the exception to the rule. I was still struggling with the new trigger weight, still battling my bad habits. For a few years after my 2008 win, I shot poorly.

In pursuit of bettering my performance, I began shooting in more events, and my calendar was full almost year round. At first, I blamed my struggles on old age. I was over 60, after all. Most of the women I was competing against were in their 20s, or even their teens. More competitions meant more travel, more practice, and more stress. It was possible all of this was taking a toll on my body.

Although I was struggling with shooting, my family life was still going well. Both Shane and Christina had married and become mothers. Shane, my younger and more artistic daughter, moved to Europe, while Christina began working for our family business. Austin was finishing school. Although he'd had some behavioral problems as an adolescent, he was improving. Austin always has been my most gifted child. He's also been incredibly stubborn. But he's brilliant, with an incredible sense of humor, and even when he struggled, I never doubted he would find his way. And he has.

Carlos and I were doing better than ever, I thought, and 2008 marked 15 years since his affair. Although I'd once been worried that the love between us might never come back, I now understood that love doesn't ever really change. The love I have for Carlos is unconditional. He's my partner and my best friend. Around 2008, I told him, "I want to marry you again in the next life. So make sure you come and find me."

Three or four days later, he said, "How am I going to find you in the next life?"

In Chinese culture, there is an old story about a pair of lovers who cannot marry. They're soul-connected, so one says, "I promise myself to you," and they break a piece of jade in two, each taking a half. When they find one another, they recognize the pieces of jade.

Carlos asked whether we should make a mark on our hands, in case we end up in two different places. We also wondered: what if we are both men or women in the next life? What if we're brother and sister? (Carlos takes a very Buddhist view on the afterlife.) No matter what happens, though, we are still connected, one way or another.

I thought about it for a few days and then said, "I don't understand everything. I'm not sure how God works on this. I'm baptized. Maybe you should get baptized, too." We talked about that for a while, but Carlos eventually decided that, because he's a good person, he thinks he'll go to heaven, too. I do, however, carry a piece of jade around – just in case.

心平

By 2011, my mother's health was failing. Her life during the previous few years had been difficult. She didn't have many people visiting her, aside from her individual caregiver. Due to the dementia, it was hard for her to make friends. Every Christmas, I'd bring gifts for the entire home, saying they were from Stella. I wanted to make her some friends. When I was a kid, Mom always talked about paving the road for me – giving special gifts to certain people, so they'd look out for me. I viewed these Christmas gifts as paving the road for her.

I went to visit her most weeks, and I came on every holiday, armed with gifts and flowers. I wanted people to see that she was valued.

In those last few years, she wasn't very communicative. I'd sit down and tell her stories. I'd tell her about my grandkids and what they were doing. It was hard for me. My mother and I could always talk for hours. Before she went into the assisted living center, we'd get dinner and talk, talk, talk. Then she'd say, "Vera, you want to go see a movie?" She knew I loved movies, so of course I'd say yes. She'd fall asleep during the film, snoring right next to me. But it was special just having her there.

I learned so much from my mother, but above all, I learned kindness and perseverance. She taught me to treat everyone with respect. When Christina asked me what was the one thing she should teach her kids, I told her, "Kindness," because that's what my mother taught me. She helped me understand that kindness allows you to see the good in the world. And she believed that this goodness passes into another person's understanding of you. If you're an honest person, people will know. Kindness permeates everything.

She was kind, but tough. Whenever I was scared, she'd say, "What's the worst that can happen to you? You're not going to die from this. So just do it." And she guided by example. I never saw her afraid or hesitant. I was surprised when she once told me, "Life is mostly hardship. It's more hardship than happiness." She never showed this in her own life, because she was mostly cheerful.

But, of course, she did suffer. She'd never gone to college, even though she was a very intelligent woman. From what Carlos and I have pieced together of her previous life, she lived much of her early adult years on the run, probably in fear. She lost her entire family, all of her roots. And even her new life wasn't perfect. She suffered through my father's affairs. While she did her best to hide it, she'd felt hurt for me when Carlos had his affair. Her heart ached for all the suffering her kids went through. Years later, she gave me the letters she'd written Carlos but never sent.

In March 2011, my mother went into a coma. All she could do was call out my name. It reminded me of being in high school. When I was leaving the house, I'd call upstairs, "Bye, Mommy." I just wanted to hear her call back, "Bye, Chavi," which was her nickname for me.

When she passed later in March, I prepared everything at the funeral. Preparation helps me control my emotions. Still, there was only so much I could do to keep my feelings from coming to the surface. My children had never seen me cry, because I usually cry at odd times, not when everyone else is crying. Simple and benign things, like movies, make me cry. But as I watched my mom's casket being taken away for burial, I thought, oh my God, I'll never see her again. I tried to pull myself together, but all I wanted to do was run after it and ask them to stop, to let her stay. I couldn't help but break into tears.

A few weeks later, I was in Columbia, preparing for the Bianchi Cup. I only told one other shooter about my mother's death, but he must have told others. One of the other top female shooters, Julie Golob, came up to me and said, "Vera, let me show you something." She took me to the moving target controls, where there was this big, beautiful moth on the wall.

"Isn't that beautiful?" she said.

And it was. I appreciated that kindness. It reminded me of my mother's.

AN UNEXPECTED CHALLENGE

In 2012, I was still struggling in competitions. Thanks to some advice from another shooter, I began to understand just what my bad habits were. I've always done things my way. This is true of all sport shooters, to some extent. We all think *our* way is the best. But my way has developed over decades of watching the greatest shooters in the world, of listening to them and trying everything, to see what works and what doesn't. When I shoot the barricade event, where you shoot at the targets while standing behind barricades, I stand on my tiptoes. It looks hideous. But I've learned from years of windsurfing and skiing that this is how I can leverage my weight to keep the gun from bouncing off the edge of the barricade. I need that extra leverage, because I'm not as strong as most of the male shooters.

Unfortunately, you can know what's wrong with your technique and still struggle to fix it. When you get into a competition, your body reverts to what it knows, to what's comfortable. And if you've spent five years getting comfortable with some bad habits, it's hard to break them.

心平

Shortly before the 2012 World Action Pistol Championship, which was once again taking place in Phillipsburg, Germany, Carlos was helping me book my flights. I was concerned about going. I'd had a very poor year shooting. But I'd been chosen to represent the U.S. team, and it was an honor to be selected. Despite doubting myself, I was going to go over there and represent my country.

While finalizing arrangements, I was on Carlos' phone. He'd left his email open, and I noticed an email from a woman I didn't recognize. She was a Chinese woman.

As I read the email, my head began to spin. Chills went through my body. I felt like I was falling down a hole, right back to the spring of 1993. I couldn't believe what was happening. I was in his study, and when I walked past him, I looked at him like he was a stranger. He was using all his strength to help me, and he was still doing something like this?

I went to Christina's house and called one of Carlos's best friends. I wanted to ask if he knew anything about this woman, but he said he didn't. After that phone call, I went home, but I decided I wasn't going to talk to Carlos until the following morning. As we've gotten older, we need more sleep than we once did. I knew if we started to talk, it would be an all-night conversation.

In the morning, I asked him about the email. For a split second, he showed me a face that I'd only seen once before: when we went to China on a business trip 20-some years ago. When Carlos is in China, he's different. He wears his coat differently, he walks differently, he even talks differently. He assumes the role of a traditional Chinese man. And for a split second, his response to my question was almost disbelief. It was like he thought, "So what? What's the big deal?"

That face? It's not the Carlos I've known all my life. But it's the influence of that traditional culture, which tells men they're the masters, that they can do whatever they want.

That look disappeared pretty quickly. He said there was no physical relationship between the two of them, so I didn't have to worry. After that, he didn't want to discuss it, so I went to my home range to practice. With the World Championships coming up, I needed to work through some of my bad habits, but considering everything that had happened with Carlos, my practice was lousy. Instead of shooting for hours, I cut practice short and went to see a movie.

Carlos isn't the kind of man to have a fight. He doesn't like confrontations, so I had to decide what I was going to do on my own – both about our marriage and about shooting at the World Championships. I talked to Christina, who works for our family business and is very close with Carlos. I told her, "I'm going to leave."

She said, "I know, but why don't you just stay? You can just take more trips, go shoot more." Our children don't know that Carlos and I aren't absentee spouses; we still spent – and spend – a lot of quality time together. We go out for dinner, for coffee; we talk for hours. We genuinely like each other's company.

Christina also was worried about the trust Carlos and I had created for our children. She didn't know what would happen to the trust if Carlos and I split up.

After talking to Christina, I called my best friend Cecilia, who told me that if I left, Austin would never get married.

I thought about this for a long time. The first affair had been very hard on Austin. I was worried that if Carlos and I got divorced, he might never trust a relationship. He once said something like, "I guess affairs just happen." That left a big impression on me. I didn't want him thinking marriage was just something you throw away.

A few days later, we had a big family dinner, with my daughter's children present. We all acted like things were OK, because we didn't want the grandkids to know what was going on. Carlos is normally very gregarious; he tells a lot of stories. But that night, he was different. He was much quieter.

A couple of days later, I was supposed to leave for Mickey Fowler's ranch, to continue my training for the World Championships. I needed to talk to Carlos before I left. I needed to tell him I was seriously considering leaving our marriage. Twenty years before, I'd told Carlos that if the same thing happened again, I would leave immediately. I'm not the kind to bluff. I do what I say. When I told Carlos this, he reassured me that he would be there to talk whenever I wanted – and that he wanted us to talk.

At the ranch, I was a mess. I was shooting terribly and having a very hard time focusing. I was constantly texting Carlos. He told me I could come home at any point. In fact, he knew how much of a mess I was. He didn't think I'd do well in Germany. He said, "Tell them you're sick. Don't go." My daughter and son-in-law agreed with him. They didn't see how I could possibly compete in Germany.

I knew shooting at the World Championship match was going to be an enormous feat. I had no self-confidence. My training sessions had been disasters. Still, I thought, "It's an honor to be chosen for this. I need to go."

Instead of sitting around wallowing in self-pity, I went to Germany to compete. I figured that if I started to fall apart, I could always go home. To keep myself feeling positive, I got the nicest suite in our hotel. I filled the room with flowers. I took care of myself and tried my best to focus. I was praying constantly, asking God to be with me, to show me the way.

I was especially concerned about the mover, which is, again, when you shoot at a target, mounted on a rail, which moves laterally at a speed of 10 feet per second, for a total of six seconds. You shoot from 10, 15, 20, and 25 yards. From each distance, the target will first move from right to left, and then back from left to right. You take six shots in each direction from the first two distances, and then three shots in each direction from the last two distances.

I'd been struggling mightily with this stage, and to make things more difficult, I was using a slightly different gun in Germany than I normally used at the Bianchi Cup. The trigger was ever so slightly lighter, at 2.125 pounds of pressure. If I pressed too hard, I'd squeeze out a shot when I wasn't ready. I spent hours dry firing in my room, telling myself, "Squeeze, squeeze; keep your arms straight."

Normally, this kind of thinking will ruin you. But I was praying nonstop, putting my trust in God. I would visualize myself in a garden with Jesus. I'd take deep breaths and picture that garden, and I'd feel happy and free. I could feel God's strength moving through me. I knew it wasn't my own strength. I wasn't strong enough to be there on my own.

During the practical stage of the competition, I ran into my first disaster. The match organizers were running behind schedule due to equipment problems, so no one competing knew when they were supposed to shoot. I went up at the time my lineup was supposed to shoot, and the woman in charge told me that we weren't up yet. I went over two more times, and each time I was told we weren't up yet.

The fourth time I went up, I was distraught to find out my group already had shot. Normally, if you miss your group, it's an automatic disqualification. But the woman knew I'd checked with her three times, and due to the messed-up schedule, they'd shot without me. So she immediately slotted me in with another lineup. This presented its own problems, as I was told that one of the shooters was using a .22 and was going to be reloading at the line, which meant we all had to wait while he did so. I was concerned that this small delay was going to further compromise my concentration. Despite the potential for distraction, I was praying to God and was fiercely engaged in concentrating. In the end, I managed to do well.

However, if I thought the practical was bad, I was worried the mover could be even worse. Due to my years-long struggles on the mover, I wanted to make sure I was as focused as possible for this stage.

Normally at big events like this, there is a safe area where shooters can handle their guns without ammo. You also can use the area to dry fire. On the day of the mover, the organizers had designated a different safe area from the one they had been using the day before.

I went to the safe area to dry fire, a form of practice where you draw the gun without live firing it. When I got there, I found a couple of shooters engaged in deep conversation. I didn't think it was a good idea to interrupt. I had seen other shooters dry firing in the previous safe areas, and they had told me this was acceptable. Over the previous two days, I'd followed all the safety instructions, and had run from place to place to dry fire before my events. Because it seemed OK to find an empty and safe space and dry fire there, I went to a place where no one was around, with a high berm, and started dry firing.

All of a sudden, someone was screaming at me to stop. I did.

A few minutes later, I was at the line, ready to shoot. I'd been knocked out of my deep focus, but I was trying to prepare. Right before I was to shoot, the range officer asked me to stop. He said we needed to speak with a match director.

While we waited, I tried hard to stay focused. It wasn't easy.

When the match director finally arrived, the range officer said he wanted to disqualify me for a safety violation. Apparently, you weren't supposed to dry fire where I'd been doing it. I didn't know this was a problem, due to what the other shooters had told me. I explained this to the match director. I hadn't done anything outright dangerous, but the range officer kept insisting I be disqualified. He even pulled out his rules booklet.

Thankfully, the match director didn't agree with him and he let me shoot. Despite this, my focus was about to get further tested. As we were about to shoot, the equipment failed.

Standing at the line, I took deep breaths. I kept my eyes focused on the spot just in front of my boots, blocking out all activity. I was asking God to help me stay focused, despite all the distractions.

Finally, after they repaired the equipment, we got to shoot.

I shot with so much anxiety. When I finished the mover, the Championship's last event, I kept my eyes closed before the range officer brought over my target for viewing. I was afraid of how many points I'd dropped. But when I looked, I was surprised: Despite all the stress and mishaps, I only dropped 13 out of 480 points. I was amazed.

At the banquet, I wore my light turquoise Chinese dress. In the open category, our team of four shooters – three women and one man – had won bronze, and my partner, Helen Jeavon, and I had won gold in the women's team division. I also won bronze as an individual in the women's division. Considering all that went wrong and all the distractions, this was an incredible result for me. A photographer captured me smiling at the event, and looking at the photo, I can't believe I was 66 at the time. The photographer said I looked radiant. And I did. With everything going on in my life, and at my age, this was my happiest win.

When I returned home from Germany, I felt better. The bit of distance had allowed me to see that, despite his flaws, Carlos has been an extraordinary gift to me. Many of my friends had husbands who didn't support them in their pursuits, and Carlos always, without hesitation, supported me. He's been a treasure in so many ways. He'd hurt me, but I understand no one is perfect. It's hard to imagine anyone I would've rather spent my life with.

A WOMAN IN A MAN'S WORLD

From the outside, some people might look at the 2012 World Championships as my last great achievement in sport shooting. After all, I hadn't won the Bianchi Cup since 2008. And less than a year later, I'd break my leg while preparing for the 2013 Bianchi Cup.

But to me, shooting has never been about wins or losses. It's been about the way the sport shapes you as a person – the way you have to be stronger, more disciplined, and more focused to shoot your best. It's not about the people you're shooting against. It's about *you* – the things you're bringing to the range, the disappointments and hopes, and your ability to set those aside. Shooting competitively is about facing challenges. Time and again, the sport has taught me how to get up after I fall.

So when I stepped onto the range in Columbia, Missouri, for the 2014 Bianchi Cup, I knew I wasn't going to win my first title in six years. I knew I wasn't going to be best newcomer. I wasn't going to be leaving with any kind of prize. But then, most people don't go to the range because they expect to win anything. We all hope to enjoy the challenge and the journey in self-discovery. Most of us that come back over and over are workaholics. We have that kind of rare total focus where we can walk off the range knowing that we shot the absolute best we could – and have that be enough.

My presence at the Bianchi Cup was against all odds. I was 67, and I'd shattered my leg. I'd grown up a Chinese-American woman in a family and culture that valued the old, traditional ways of life. And yet, in May 2014, there I was, ready to shoot. I was there because I didn't want to miss an opportunity to participate in another Bianchi Cup. Because I wanted to test my strength and ability to persevere. I wanted to put into practice the words "never give up."

And I was also there because my mother had taught me what it is to live a life of kindness. Because my son, Bryan, had taught me how to get through unimaginable pain. Because Carlos has supported me, through thick and thin, and has always remained my partner.

Above all, I was there because God has a plan for us. That plan isn't always easy, but God is there every step of the way. And although we may not always see it, God is in every molecule of everything. If we're listening to God's plan, if we're looking for His presence, anything is possible.

I like to think the sport-shooting world has changed over my time in the sport – that more and more women are involved in it. But I know it's still a male-dominated world. But then, so many worlds are still male-dominated.

I realize that, as one of the prominent female shooters in the sport – and a prominent Chinese-American woman – I'm a bit of a rarity from my generation. I hope I'll serve as an example to women from all backgrounds: that they can look at my story and see shooting can be a great sport for women. Since most women don't have much experience shooting, they tend to be blank slates. This means it's easier to take instruction, especially in a sport like target shooting. I hope more women get into the sport, as it builds self-esteem and discipline. Even if you don't shoot competitively, knowing gun safety and understanding how to shoot well are great skills to have.

Sport shooting competitions are interesting to observe. All that you are as a person – the good things, the flaws, the preoccupations – shows up in a match. If you're going to be serious about shooting, very early on, you have to clean house with yourself. Whatever issues you have inside will show up in a match. Through my matches, I came to discover what I am and what I am not. It pays to be true to who you are.

Just as sport shooting will expose your flaws, it also will highlight your strengths. This sport brought out who I am. I have a lot of endurance and emotional stamina. I was trained for this through the difficulties I had with my in-laws. I'm also hard-working, and this was exercised through the family business: If we hadn't worked hard, we would've gone bankrupt. Shooting has utilized the many and varied skills I developed over the years.

Ultimately, I believe that competitive shooting is a good metaphor for life. You face adversity, but it won't ruin you. If you have a bad day shooting, you can still go home, regroup, come back, and try again next time. This is true of adversity in life, too. We have to remember never to give up and to value those moments when we get a second chance.

Competitive shooting also helps you build goals. You can't just say, "I'm going to be a world-champion shooter." It's too much work, and you'll break under the weight of it. So you start out with a realistic goal, and when you achieve it, you make a new goal. This is how you become a world champion: not by setting out to be one, but by setting, and achieving, one small goal after another. Through shooting, you learn what you're made of. The sport is about self-discovery.

I also hope that women who have struggled can look at my life and see that painful events don't have to be destructive forces. When I think back on how I felt when I found out about Carlos' affair, it was like a bomb had gone off in my life. But I see now that God allowed that bomb to explode so I could use that energy to change my life. Instead of becoming a ticking bomb myself, I harnessed that destructive energy and directed it toward something productive. For me, it was competitive shooting. But honestly, it could have been anything. Pain, betrayal, and difficulty don't have to destroy you. They can make you stronger.

I don't think the men who've said things to me, or looked at me like I don't belong, quite understood just how I much I really *didn't* belong in their world – or how unlikely my success has been. I grew up in a traditional Chinese household, where women were expected to attend to their husbands before pursuing any of their own dreams. A woman in that culture wasn't supposed to be able to have a family *and* achieve feats of her own in the world. Stepping out of that culture and becoming one of the best shooters in the world is something I wouldn't have thought possible. But the fact that I did it shows it's possible to do just about anything if you work hard enough, put your trust in God's plan, and refuse to let people stop you.

ACHIEVEMENTS

©Jack Hutcheson

Championships

- Gold medal, women's division, at the 1996 American Handgunner World Shoot-off Championship, Montrose, Colorado.
- 1999 Top Women's Team at the NRA World Action Pistol Championship in Hamilton, New Zealand; as a member of

the U.S. Women's Team, Vera competed with teammate Julie Golob.

- Gold medal in the women's division at the 1999, 2001, 2002, 2003, 2004, 2005, 2006 and 2008 NRA National Action Pistol (Bianchi) Championship, Columbia, Missouri.
- Gold medal in the women's division at the 1999 European Action Pistol Championship, Tierney, Italy.
- Gold medal, Women's Team, at the 2012 NRA World Action Pistol Championship in Philippsburg, Germany. Vera competed with teammate Helen Jeavon. Vera also captured the bronze medal in the Women's Division at the World Championship as part of the U.S. National Shooting Team, the first time the U.S. team included female members in the Open Category. The other members of the team were Ms. Jessie Duff, Ms. Julie Golob and Mr. Kim Beckwith.
- Gold medal at the 2010 NRA World Action Pistol Championship in Blacktown, Australia. Vera competed with teammate Julie Golob. Vera also captured second place in the Women's Category at the World Championship as part of the USA National Shooting Team.
- Gold medal, Individual Award, at the 2004 NRA World Action Pistol Championship; Columbia, Missouri.
- Gold medal at the 2007 NRA National Action Pistol Championship in Columbia, Missouri.
- Gold medal in the women's division at the 2007 European Open/Action Pistol Championship, Phillippsburg, Germany.
- Gold medal, women's division, at the 2004 and 2005 Master's Championship, Barry, Illinois.

- Gold medal in the women's division at the 2003 Regional Action Pistol Championship, Kansas City, Missouri.
- Bronze medal, Women's Team, at the 2018 NRA World Action Pistol Championship in Hallsville, Missouri. Vera competed with teammate Jessie Harrison.

Records

- Vera set a women's record in 1997 for highest score in the Practical Event at the National Action Pistol Championship in Columbia, Missouri. Her score was 480-40X.
- Vera has been recognized for setting a national record for top score by a woman on the outdoor action pistol Crawford Barricade, in San Antonio, Texas, on October 8, 2005. She shot 480-45X.
- In September 2006, Vera set a national record for women's score and senior's score in the Barricade Event, 480-43X.
- In November 2010, Vera was recognized for setting a national Senior record in the outdoor action pistol Modified Mover-AP Target, Open Sights, shooting 461-26X; and a national Women's record in the outdoor action pistol Moving-AP Target, shooting 223-10X.
- In August 2011, Vera was recognized for co-holding a national record for senior's score in the Falling Plate Event, 480-48X.
- Vera set a national record for women's score in the Combat Event, shooting a 578, in September 2011.
- Vera has been recognized for setting a national record for women's score in the Practical Event, 480-35X, in October 2011.

- In September 2015, Vera set a national record for women's score in the Texas Mover-AP Target, shooting 466-23X.
- In April 2016, Vera was recognized for setting a national Grand Senior record for her score in the Barricade Event, 480-45X; Modified Moving Target, 462-25X; Falling Plate Event, 460-46X; and the Practical Event, 480-32X.
- In November 2017, Vera was recognized for setting a national Grand Senior record in the outdoor action pistol Modified Moving Target Event, Optical Sights, shooting 462-26X.
- Vera Koo was a member of the United States World Action Pistol Shooting Team from 1999 through 2018.

Made in the USA
Middletown, DE
16 June 2022

67252629R00113